TRAGIC BEING

· TRAGIC BEING ·

APOLLO AND DIONYSUS IN
WESTERN DRAMA

by N. *JOSEPH CALARCO*

THE UNIVERSITY OF MINNESOTA PRESS

Minneapolis

Library of Congress Catalog Card Number: 68-55801

PUBLISHED IN GREAT BRITAIN, INDIA, AND PAKISTAN BY THE OXFORD UNIVERSITY
PRESS, LONDON, BOMBAY, AND KARACHI, AND IN CANADA BY THE COPP CLARK
PUBLISHING CO. LIMITED, TORONTO

The section on *The Screens*, pages 169–176, was first published as "Vision without Compromise: Genet's *The Screens*" in *Drama Survey*, IV, No. 1 (Spring,
1965), 44–50, and appears here by permission of the publisher. Lines quoted
from "Lapis Lazuli" are reprinted with permission of The Macmillan Company,
New York; The Macmillan Company of Canada; and A. P. Watt & Sons from
Collected Poems by W. B. Yeats. Copyright 1940 by Georgie Yeats. Lines quoted
from "From the 'Antigone'" and "Three Movements" are reprinted with permission of The Macmillan Company, New York; The Macmillan Company of Canada; and A. P. Watt & Sons from *Collected Poems* by W. B. Yeats. Copyright
1933 by The Macmillan Company renewed 1961 by Bertha Georgie Yeats. Ex-
cerpts from Henrik Ibsen's *The Master Builder* are from *Six Plays*, translated by
Eva Le Gallienne (New York: Random House (Modern Library), 1951, 1957),
and are reprinted with permission of Random House, Inc., and Brandt & Brandt.

For Margot

· PREFACE ·

THIS book is an exploration of the hidden order beyond tragedy's visible circle of action and suffering, and of the value which that order assigns to human existence.

The focus of my attention is a set of plays central to the history of Western drama. They are examined with the aid of two sets of related concepts, for whose formulation I am indebted to Friedrich Nietzsche and Mircea Eliade. First is the Apollonian/Dionysiac duality, which supplies a profoundly relevant vocabulary for discussing both the concrete tensions of tragic dramas and their philosophical implications. Because tragedy has assumed varied forms since its Hellenic origins, I shall speak of it historically; but a discussion of tragedy *in* history is not sufficient. More basic are the ideas of history's relation to man which tragedy has embodied. They will be examined in terms of a second duality, whose poles are the anhistorical and historical visions of man.

The Introduction presents and defines these basic concepts and discusses some of their implications. The body of the work begins with an analysis of the *Oresteia* and proceeds to plays by Sophocles and Euripides. The central chapter on *King Lear* is followed by briefer discussions of plays by Racine, Hebbel, Ibsen, Brecht, and Genet.

It is of course impossible to represent adequately the whole scope of tragedy in a dozen works by nine playwrights. My goal has been rather to direct attention to certain crucial *moments* in its development, plays which have posed the tragic dilemma in particularly vivid and forceful terms. I shall be happy if I have managed to indicate one possible approach to a genre which has added much to an understanding of man's position in the universe.

An earlier version of the discussion of Genet appeared in *Drama Survey*, which has kindly granted permission for its use. I wish to thank Arthur H. Ballet for his aid and encouragement in the early stages of this book's preparation, and John Dennis Hurrell, Robert Sonkowsky, Marvin Rosenberg, Robert W. Goldsby, and Travis Bogard for their helpful suggestions. I remain indebted to Robert Brustein for his early inspiration as a teacher and for the important lesson of boldness. Much of what is best here is due to these men; the defects are entirely my own.

Finally, I wish to thank my wife, Margot Demarais Calarco, for her aid in the preparation of the manuscript, and more significantly, her patience and loving support in the most difficult midnight hours of its composition.

N. J. C.

Wayne State University
Detroit, Michigan

· TABLE OF CONTENTS ·

TRAGIC BEING

·INTRODUCTION·

TRAGEDY AND HISTORY

All things fall and are built again,
And those that build them again are gay.
W. B. YEATS, "Lapis Lazuli"

IN THE period preceding the Second World War, William Butler
Yeats wrote a poem about tragedy in life and literature. "Lapis
Lazuli" begins with his mockery of those "hysterical women," the
modern prophets of doom who fear "That if nothing drastic is
done/ Aeroplane and Zeppelin will come out,/ Pitch like King
Billy bomb-balls in/ Until the town lie beaten flat." The poem
proceeds to the recognition of a calmer truth—"Hamlet and Lear
are gay;/ Gaiety transfiguring all that dread."[1] Yet the gaiety of
these tragic heroes is not a reflection of their status as immortal
artifacts. The work of art shares in the mortality of all civilizations,
which must fall and will be rebuilt.

The inevitable destruction of men and their creations is an article
of modern faith; we are not likely to question it. But like the
hysterical women, and fearing weapons more terrible than aeroplane or Zeppelin, we may doubt the possibility of new beginnings
in life and art. To the extent that we accept the uniqueness of the
historical event, irretrievable after its moment of potency, we deny
Yeats' metaphysical solace.

"Lapis Lazuli" does more than reveal the difference between a poetic faith and a version of the modern temper. It focuses our attention on the radical difference between two sets of cultural attitudes—attitudes which, in varying forms and during different phases of Western civilization, have attended the human rituals of life and death and their image in tragic art.

Mircea Eliade names and discusses these attitudes and their ontological significance in *Cosmos and History*.[2] There is, declares Eliade, a significant difference between "archaic" (or "anhistorical") societies and modern "historical" society. The difference does not lie in the negative connotations of the word "archaic"; anhistorical man is not necessarily more naive, more primitive than historical man. Rather, archaic societies are distinguished by "their revolt against concrete, historical time, their nostalgia for a periodical return to the mythical time of the beginning of things."[3] Historical man sees the individual event as a datum shorn of transhistorical meaning; when archaic man regards events,

their meaning, their value, are not connected with their crude physical datum but with the property of reproducing a primordial act, of repeating a mythical example. Nutrition is not a simple physiological operation; it renews a communion. Marriage and the collective orgy echo mythical prototypes; they are repeated because they were consecrated in the beginning ("in those days," *in illo tempore, ab origine*) by gods, ancestors, or heroes.[4]

There is intrinsic in this "rejection of profane, continuous time, a certain metaphysical 'valorization' of human existence."[5] Even the death of men, of works of art, of civilizations, becomes coherent and meaningful in this perspective. Yeats' affirmation that "all things fall and are built again" is not a sad acknowledgment of man's need to painfully rebuild what has been destroyed; rather, it reflects the insight that

any form whatever, by the mere fact that it exists as such and endures, necessarily loses vigor and becomes worn; to recover vigor, it must be reabsorbed into the formless if only for an instant; it must be restored to the primordial unity from which it issued; in other words, it must return to "chaos" (on the cosmic plane), to "orgy" (on the social plane), to "darkness" (for seed).[6]

The movement from life to death to resurrection, the transition from order to chaos and back to order, can be understood on all planes—the cosmic as well as the human, the biological as well as the historical. Time itself has a cyclical structure, "which is regenerated at each new 'birth' on whatever plane. This eternal return reveals an ontology uncontaminated by time and becoming." [7] The archaic, the anhistorical war is more than the clash of ignorant armies by night, and the sufferings of all anhistorical Hamlets have a meaningful relation to joy, to order restored, to form achieved amid the seeming tumults of existence.

The anhistorical view of reality is not the exclusive property of "primitive" cultures, though it may be one of their dominant characteristics. As Eliade observes, we find this "reduction of events to categories and of individuals to archetypes, carried out by the consciousness of the popular strata in Europe almost down to our day." [8] If such tendencies manifest themselves in popular legend, we should not be surprised to find them also nourishing the roots of tragic drama, which, even its most poetically and structurally sophisticated examples, has an uncommon ability to reflect levels of culture beneath what is currently fashionable in court or city or among the intellectual élite.

Yet tragedy feeds on irony, on paradox, whereas archaic ontology provides a ready-made resolution of all contradictions and a determinate scheme in which the value of action and event are invariable. Although we shall find in the course of this study that tragedy reflects (on one level) an archaic ontology, we shall also discover that tragedies cannot be interpreted as unqualified expressions of this ontology.

Furthermore, it will be necessary to free the notion of "archetype" from theories about the *origins* of tragedy such as those advanced by Nietzsche or the Cambridge anthropologists. These theories remain highly speculative,[9] and are, in any case, external to a direct experience of the tragic play. When I speak of an archetype in the following chapters, I will be referring to a transhistoric model for the actions, gestures, or passions of individual characters —a model behind the visible scene which is part of the metaphysical context of the tragedy and which helps to define the "eternal," atemporal shape of its particular and temporal action.

Apollo and Dionysus: The Tragic Paradox

Eliade's thesis leads to the central question of this book—the question of tragic ontology. What is the nature of the tragic "valorization" of human existence and, in particular, human suffering? Can we say that tragic man, like historical man, *is* to the extent that he "makes himself, within history"?[10] Or is his being drawn, like that of archaic man, from his repetition of archetypal gestures? Is his position to be found somewhere between these extremes? Finally, is it possible that we err in speaking of "tragic man" without accounting for the vast differences between the periods in which tragedy has been written, and the vast differences between tragic writers? Surely, the answers to such questions can be reached only through a careful examination of major works in the tradition, considered in their historic and philosophic context.

A tool is required for such a study—a working conceptual vocabulary which is capable of accounting for the complexities and seeming contradictions of the tragic experience. Such a vocabulary is to be found in the eloquent though sometimes erratic pages of Friedrich Nietzsche's early masterpiece, *The Birth of Tragedy*. Nietzsche's terminology—and its metaphysical assumptions—is what will be of concern here. His speculations about the historical origins of Greek tragedy are less valuable than his insight into the impulses and tensions that give birth to a tragic art.

Nietzsche discerns two formative influences on tragedy in ancient Greece, two artistic and cultural principles—the Apollonian and the Dionysiac. They stand in much the same relation to each other as *dream* and *intoxication*, and find their characteristic expression in the plastic arts and music, respectively. The dream sphere of Apollonian art is *not* a post-Freudian realm of nightmare, but rather a realm of "fair illusion," of "deep delight." Here "we enjoy an immediate apprehension of form, all shapes speak to us directly, nothing seems indifferent or redundant." Over this realm Apollo reigns, who is "at once the god of all plastic powers and the soothsaying god. He who is etymologically the 'lucent' one, the god of light, reigns also over . . . our inner world of fantasy." Furthermore,

the perfection of these conditions in contrast to our imperfectly understood waking reality, as well as our profound awareness of nature's healing power during the interval of sleep and dream, furnishes a symbolic analogue to the soothsaying faculty and quite generally to the arts, which make life possible and worth living. But the image of Apollo must incorporate that thin line which the dream image must not cross, under penalty of becoming pathological, of imposing itself on us as crass reality: a discreet limitation, a freedom from all extravagant urges, the sapient tranquility of the plastic god.[11]

Therefore the Apollonian is associated with balance, order, the avoidance of extremes; it is the aesthetic equivalent of the ethical golden mean of Aristotle. It has, then, both a positive and a negative content—it fulfills the human need for tranquil illusion while avoiding the cruel and orgiastic urges of mankind.

This sketch of Apollo's dream sphere is completed with the aid of a passage from Schopenhauer's *The World as Will and Idea*:

"Even as on an immense, raging sea, assailed by huge wave crests, a man sits in a little rowboat trusting his frail craft, so, amidst the furious torments of this world, the individual sits tranquilly, supported by the *principium individuationis* and relying on it." One might say that the unshakeable confidence in that principle has received its most magnificent expression in Apollo, and that Apollo himself may be regarded as the marvelous divine image of the *principium individuationis*.[12]

If the plastic illusion of dream is the aesthetic aspect of the Apollonian, its philosophical aspect is the "principle of individuation," which may be defined as "the intrinsic, real factor in an existing singular thing which causes the individuality of the thing."[13]

The *principium individuationis* can best be understood when compared with its opposite. Nietzsche describes

the tremendous awe which seizes man when he suddenly begins to doubt the cognitive modes of experience, in other words, when in a given instance the law of causation seems to suspend itself. If we add to this awe the glorious transport which arises in man, even from the very depths of nature, at the shattering of the *principium individuationis*, then we are in a position to apprehend the essence of Dionysiac rapture, whose closest analogy is furnished by physical intoxication.[14]

Nietzsche's second principle, the *Dionysiac*, is tied to ecstasy and an awe beyond cognition, extremes beyond "that thin line" which the Apollonian dream image must not cross. It is significant that he cites physical intoxication as the closest analogy to the Dionysiac state. There is a sense in which the intoxicated man has withdrawn from contact with others, that is, from contact with them insofar as they are *individuals*. Through this withdrawal, the individual features of "the other" are annihilated. If the reveler has a wench on his lap, he has forgotten her name, her station, perhaps even the color of her eyes, and the mouth which he kisses is the mouth of all women.

It is this celebrant, not a social rebel, which we should see in Nietzsche's description of Dionysiac man:

Now the slave emerges as a freeman; all the rigid, hostile walls which either necessity or despotism has erected between men are shattered. Now that the gospel of universal harmony is sounded, each individual becomes not only reconciled to his fellow but actually at one with him—as though the veil of Maya had been torn apart and there remained only shreds floating before the vision of mystical Oneness.[15]

The boundaries between individuals are shattered, but individuation must itself be shattered to make this possible. Man is united to man, but only insofar as both merge into Oneness, the universal ground of Being. In this state, man is united with nature as well as his fellow: "The earth offers its gifts voluntarily, and the savage beasts of mountain and desert approach in peace." Each of man's gestures "betokens enchantment; through him sounds a supernatural power, the same power which makes the animals speak and the earth render up milk and honey."[16] These are the triumphant visions of Dionysiac man.

Yet beneath these visions, and those of the Apollonian state, sits "truth and its terror." Behind the Dionysiac aesthetic event lies a "terrible witches' brew concocted of lust and cruelty"; and the emotions of Dionysiac man "hark back (as the medicinal drug harks back to the deadly poison) to the days when the infliction of pain was experienced as joy."[17] Even *Apollonian* culture "must always triumph first over titans, kill monsters, and overcome the sober contemplation of actuality, the intense susceptibility to suffering, by means of illusions strenuously and zestfully entertained." Apollonian man's will to remain on earth, his identification with existence, cause him to turn his lament to "a song of praise."[18] The satyr Silenus, companion to Dionysus, utters the harsh wisdom that makes the song's illusion necessary: "What would be best for you is quite beyond your reach: not to have been born, not to *be*, to be *nothing*. But the second best is to die soon."[19]

Both the Apollonian and the Dionysiac illusions — the first serene, the second ecstatic—rise as affirmations from this background of suffering and cruelty. Nietzsche speaks of their "discordant concord," and of that "thaumaturgy of an Hellenic act of will" by which they "accepted the yoke of marriage, and, in that condition, begot Attic tragedy, which exhibits the salient features of both parents."[20] Tragedy involves a paradoxical union of opposed illusions whose purpose is to place man beyond naked, unmediated suffering, and beyond the despair which he feels when suffering can neither be ignored nor made intelligible in some context larger than the individual experience of pain.

Nietzsche is speaking, of course, of Attic tragedy, and his principles bear the names of Greek gods. Yet he admits Shakespeare and (though he will later regret the choice) Wagner into his tragic pantheon.[21] We are therefore justified in exploring the Apollonian and Dionysiac tendencies in *all* of Western tragic drama. Such a study must, however, rest on the recognition that each of the two principles is itself *composite.* Nietzsche sees tragedy as the wedding of the Apollonian and the Dionysiac. Yet the Apollonian weds a realm of "fair illusion" to the *principium individuationis* which may, under different circumstances, posit a radical alienation of individual man from the world, together with the despair which proceeds from such alienation. And the Dionysiac shattering of the

principle of individuation may become a loss of identity far removed from Dionysiac ecstasy. The importance of these tendencies will become increasingly clear in the chapters to follow.

Tragic Ontology

Is there a specifically *tragic* conception of being, a tragic framework for the ontological valorization of human existence? More
specifically: What metaphysical valorizations of existence are implied by the Dionysiac and Apollonian mentalities, and how do
they combine in tragedy?

Dionysiac man merges into mystical Oneness, the ground of
Being where the harmony between man and man, and between
man and nature, is sounded. Nietzsche also speaks of "the vir-
gins who . . . move solemnly toward the temple of Apollo," re-
taining their identities and their civic names, and contrasts them
with the "chorus of the transformed, who have forgotten their civic
past and social rank, who have become timeless servants of their
god."[22] Dionysiac man, like Eliade's archaic man, is separated by a
chasm from quotidian reality. If the chorus "depicts reality more
truthfully and more completely than does civilized man, who ordi-
narily considers himself the only reality,"[23] what is depicted is anhistorical, not historical reality. The actions and suffering of Nietzsche's tragic hero, like those of archaic man, echo "mythical prototypes."[24]

It would seem, then, that Dionysiac man is a version of archaic
man, while Apollonian man, bound to his unique identity and
civic name, is a version of historical man who lives in "concrete
time" and retains his individual memory.[25] Yet the situation is
not quite this simple. In the course of his analysis of the Apollonian
dream state, Nietzsche makes the following observations:

Although of the two halves of life—the waking and the dreaming
—the former is generally considered not only the more important
but the only one which is truly lived, I would, at the risk of sounding paradoxical, propose the opposite view. . . . I feel inclined to
the hypothesis that the original Oneness, the ground of Being,
ever-suffering and contradictory, time and again has need of rapt

vision and delightful illusion to redeem itself. Since we ourselves are the very stuff of such illusions, we must view ourselves as the truly non-existent, that is to say, as a perpetual unfolding in time, space and causality—what we label "empiric reality."

He adds that the Apollonian work of art is "the illusion of an illusion," which, like our dreams, thereby provides "a still higher form of satisfaction of the original desire for illusion."[26]

Thus, although the Apollonian (insofar as it embraces the *principium individuationis*) seems to belong to the quotidian reality of historical culture, it also (insofar as it embraces dream and illusion) denies that reality. The Apollonian dream state is more truly lived than waking life; here man attains greater fullness of being. But waking life is an illusion of "the ground of Being," and Apollonian illusion and art attain their valorization of human existence by compounding an illusion (the dream of life) with an illusion (the dream in life). Although Nietzsche is highly critical of Socratic dialectic as expounded by Plato, his views here are, on at least one level, analogous to the vision of reality presented in *Phaedo* and Book VII of *The Republic*. Plato divides quotidian "reality" from the realm of ideal forms, the realm of becoming from the realm of being. The latter is transcendent Reality, the former "a cheat and an illusion."[27] For both Nietzsche and Plato, quotidian existence is an illusion in relation to the ground of Being.

But here the analogy between the two philosophers ends. Their differences are most striking in the value which each assigns to aesthetic creation: Plato downgrades art because it is the imitation of an imitation (the quotidian realm of appearances), but Nietzsche affirms the absolute value of an art which is "the illusion of an illusion."[28] Furthermore, this compound illusion does not represent a defective image of the ground of Being, but arises as a necessary vision *in* Being, which is "ever-suffering and contradictory." For Plato, Being is necessarily unified and tranquil; for Nietzsche, it is the source of that turbulence and paradox from which tragic art arises; and illusion is necessary to Being, the truly existent, as well as to man. Nietzsche has stood Plato's ontology on its head.

Apollonian man is not simply a version of historical man; he is, as it were, that man raised to a higher power and made ideal. Historical man, who exists "in time, space and causality," is "the very stuff of . . . illusions"—the illusions of the ground of Being; Apollonian man lives in the lovelier, more orderly "illusion of an illusion" which is the dream or work of art created in the quotidian world but transcending it. Apollonian art itself "is not an imitation of nature but its metaphysical supplement." [29] In this sense, the Apollonian is, like the Dionysiac, anhistorical, and Apollonian man is engaged in archaic man's metaphysical valorization of human existence. Yet, his dream remains *individual*, unlike Dionysiac man's absorption in his archetype and Oneness. He continues to retain this important characteristic of historical man. His individuation, however, is mediated by myth, and by the sense that individuation is associated with illusion and its transfiguration of quotidian reality.

This formulation is given added force by Nietzsche's contrast between Apollo/Dionysus and historical culture, in a passage strongly reminiscent of Eliade's basic contrast:

It may be claimed that a nation, like an individual, is valuable only insofar as it is able to give to quotidian experience the stamp of the eternal. Only by so doing can it express its profound, if unconscious, conviction of the relativity of time and the metaphysical meaning of life. The opposite begins to happen when a nation begins to view itself historically and to demolish the mythical bulwarks that surround it. [30]

Both the Apollonian and the Dionysiac stand outside the quotidian realm of historical culture; yet, as Eliade observes, "a very considerable fraction of the population of Europe, to say nothing of the other continents, still lives today by the light of the traditional, anti-'historicist' viewpoint." [31] In such a context, the duel of historical/anhistorical viewpoints may provide a significant basis for the metaphysical tensions underlying tragic conflict. Nietzsche sees these tensions at work in the background of Greek tragedy, whose two principles continually draw their anhistorical significance from the quotidian life they are intended to overcome—a life characterized by suffering, "the sober contemplation of actuality," and what Eliade calls "the terror of history."[32]

Tragedy therefore involves an exceedingly complex and unstable balance. It combines the Apollonian and Dionysiac illusions, which become mutually dependent elements of a play. At the same time, both illusions rise from a need to overcome the terrors of quotidian reality, and are therefore *dependent* upon the existence of that reality. This precarious equilibrium may be upset in two ways. Without Apollonian order, the terrors of quotidian life may manifest themselves through a primitive version of the Dionysiac, a "paroxysm of lust and cruelty."[33] Without the deep wisdom of Dionysus, the Apollonian may be transformed into superficial rationality—what Nietzsche calls "esthetic Socratism"—a version of the "sensible" side of quotidian life.[34] In either case, history has invaded that aspect of tragedy which had transcended history.

It is the purpose of this study to show that the "development" of tragic art can be described in terms of the shifting relation between historicist and anhistorical elements, between a valorization of man's existence mediated by time and one mediated by some version of eternity. *All tragedies begin with a basis in quotidian experience;* all display, furthermore, a *dualistic* metaphysical basis endemic to the Western intellectual tradition. However, the nature of that dualism and its significance for the individual have undergone various changes. The *Oresteia*, for example, posits a duel between the anhistoric Apollonian and Dionysiac principles—a duel which finally leads to a reconciliation in which both gods and men participate. In Sophocles' *Oedipus at Colonus*, the reconciliation becomes an individual rather than a collective triumph; in Euripides, there is no reconciliation. Shakespeare's *King Lear*, reflecting the stresses inherent in the medieval world-view, which combines historical and anhistorical elements, presents the reconciliation as a paradoxical, individual vision, set against the harsh negations of quotidian existence. In the philosophy of Hegel, and modern drama generally from the time of Racine, there is a transition to pure historicism, with various versions of Reason and Passion replacing Apollo and Dionysus as the tragic polarities. Modern "tragedy" reflects the limitations of historicism, and fails, on the whole, to provide an adequate valorization of the tragic hero's existence and suffering. However, tendencies toward the earlier vision are to be found in such works as Ibsen's *The Master Builder*.

A *Closing Note*: One problem must be acknowledged before I begin an analysis of particular plays with the aid of Nietzsche's terminology. The philosopher is consistent in characterizing the relation of his extreme terms: "rapt vision" (Dionysiac) and "delightful illusion" (Apollonian) both arise from a "ground of Being" which is "ever-suffering and contradictory." However, he sees the middle term—quotidian existence—alternately as "truth and its terror" and a redeeming "illusion" of the ground of Being. But Nietzsche also tells us that "both art and life depend wholly on the laws of optics . . .; both, to be blunt, depend on the necessity of error." [35] Life (like art) remains indeterminate, mysterious, irreducible to any simple formula. What we perceive in it is very much a matter of *perspective*. The hysterical women of Yeats' "Lapis Lazuli" see the terror of quotidian truth; his Chinamen, seated on their distant mountaintop, see life as an illusion. Each perception has its validity. The mournful melodies of tragedy require both.

· THE ORESTEIA ·

Up to now the most conspicuous failure of both the traditional
and the new critics in respect to Greek tragedy has been the
failure to realize turbulence: turbulence of experience, turbulence
of morality in the process of getting made, and the turbulence of
ideas under dramatic test.

WILLIAM ARROWSMITH

MUCH criticism has indeed involved the reduction of the turbulence of tragedy[1] to an intelligible system—a sequence of axioms
and propositions which are logically defensible and which imply, in
the final analysis, that the order of tragedy is not unlike that of
logical demonstration. Behind this lies the assumption, stated or
implied, that tragedy affirms what Norman DeWitt calls "a managed universe."[2] Nietzsche's *Birth of Tragedy* escapes this assumption to the extent that it displays the philosopher's avoidance of
systematic thought and his recognition of the Dionysiac turbulence
at the heart of tragedy.

However, the profundity of Nietzsche's insight into tragic duality
is not always matched by his exposition of the specific operation
of this duality in particular plays. He is, in fact, guilty of frequent
unsupported generalizations which seem to belie his recognition
of tragic turbulence. Nowhere in *The Birth of Tragedy* can we find
a detailed interpretation of any given play. I must therefore distinguish between Nietzsche's conceptual scheme (which is a tool
of this study) and his assumptions about the relation of this
scheme to Greek tragedy.

Nietzsche speaks of the "*attending* chorus" of tragedy, which waits upon the tragic protagonist, who in turn embodies the action and suffering of Dionysus. The chorus "beholds its lord and master Dionysus, . . . it sees how the god suffers and transforms himself, and it has, for that reason, no need to act."[3] Even a superficial examination of the *Oresteia* bares the inadequacies of this formulation. The Furies of the *Eumenides* are by no means followers or servants of Orestes, and they are in a sense the most malevolently *active* agents in that play. Nietzsche's view of the tragic hero as an "Apollonian embodiment" of Dionysus is equally inadequate.[4] If we examine Agamemnon, we do indeed discover a hero who suffers—but what he suffers is physical violence, and that offstage; nor is there any indication that he "transforms himself" through any act of complete tragic perception, though he is himself matter-of-factly transformed into a corpse by others.

The only character in this play to whom Nietzsche's formulation may be applied with some degree of validity is, in fact, Cassandra; and her relation to the play reveals another problem. Nietzsche speaks of the "oracular words of wisdom" characteristically uttered by the mantic chorus.[5] Yes, the chorus of *Agamemnon* is prophetic; yet there comes a moment when Agamemnon is stripping for his bath inside the palace and Cassandra utters prophecies of death and ruin which it cannot understand—both its powers of prophecy and its ability to interpret have been suspended. We find a similar situation in *The Libation Bearers*; it is not until Clytaemestra has been killed that the chorus turns from an optimistic view of the consequences of the deed; and a central point of the *Eumenides* seems to be precisely the need to transcend the limited and brutal wisdom of the Chorus of Furies.

Nietzsche contrasts "the Dionysiac poetry of the chorus, on the one hand, and the Apollonian dream world of the scene on the other." He goes on to say that "everything that rises to the surface in the Apollonian portion of Greek tragedy (in the dialogue) looks simple, transparent, beautiful."[6] Again, what are we to say of Cassandra's distracted song of death? Here it seems almost as if the Dionysiac Chorus and actor have traded functions.

These questions become particularly troublesome when we realize that they arise from an observation of the major surviving work of Aeschylus, who is closer than Sophocles or Euripides to the "birth" of tragedy. It is clear that both the order and the turbulence of the *Oresteia* are not accounted for by Nietzsche's simple polarization of tragedy into a Dionysiac Chorus and Apollonian dialogue. The Apollonian and Dionysiac principles operate in more complex ways. I hope to suggest some of this complexity through an analysis of the particulars of each play.

Agamemnon

The trilogy which will end in the full daylight of Athene's court, under Apollo's sun, begins at night. A Watchman speaks, complaining of the weariness of his quotidian existence, of his "watchtime measured by years" (1.2).[7] He is waiting for a light—a beacon "blaze of the darkness, harbinger of day's shining" (21), the sign of Agamemnon's return to Argos, harbinger of the new day of his reign, a day which will bring "redemption from distress" (19) for the Argives. The nature of this distress is not stated, but "the house itself, could it take voice, might speak" (35). The Watchman's joy at seeing the beacon flare has lapsed into a hint and silence.

The Watchman has said, "I will make my choral prelude" (30), but it is very different from the chorus which follows. Aeschylus has conveyed a great deal of specific information, and a hint of more to come, through a highly individuated character, bleary-eyed and complaining, who belongs to the workaday world. The tragedy begins with a flare, a fragment of Apollo's light, and a moment of Apollonian clarity about the meaning of that light—Agamemnon's return and the restoration of order.

Upon this temporary light breaks the Chorus in full flood, and we can hear in its song the force of Nietzsche's Dionysus. True, it is a *particular* Chorus, composed of men too old (ten years ago) to sail for Troy, but even its individuality is seen in a universal context:

> . . . beyond age, leaf
> withered, man goes three footed

no stronger than a child is,
a dream that falters in daylight.
[79–82]

The very old are "beyond age," but so are the insights of this Chorus of old men, who annihilate time and space in their song. First they sing of the departure of the Argives for Troy, telling how "their cry of war went shrill from the heart,/as eagles stricken in agony/ for young perished" (48–50). The army's triumphant war cry merges with the eagles' cry of pain, and both sound from the contradictory ground of Being. Now the battle of "the struggling masses, legs tired,/knees grinding in dust" (63–64) has begun; "Danaans and Trojans/ they have it alike" (66–67). Danaans and Trojans, and the Chorus, since man is "a dream that falters in daylight."

The Chorus turns from the eagles' nests, from Troy, from its frail age, to ask Clytaemestra about the "sweet hope" (100) in blazing altars whose flames are "staggered . . . drugged" (92, 94). Dionysus has intoxicated its vision, and from it surges "singing magic/grown to my life and power" (106–7). The "rapt vision" of the Dionysiac is very much in evidence here, and the terror of history is transcended in a vision which sees all "historical" events as examples of a single pattern of action and suffering which is not limited to a particular time or place. The Chorus has leaped from past to present—or, rather, brought both singing into its moment on the stage; now it summons the past again, and sings of a past prophecy about an act already accomplished—the sacrifice of Iphigenia. Three times, in the midst of its memories, the Chorus sings "sorrow, sorrow: but good win out in the end" (120, 139, 159). The words of hope are its moment of Apollonian illusion, "luminous spots, as it were, designed to cure an eye hurt by the ghastly night." [8]

The contradictions inherent in human action have a source beyond themselves. The Chorus addresses

Zeus, who guided men to think
who has laid it down that wisdom

comes alone through suffering.
Still there drips in sleep against the heart
grief of memory; against
our pleasure we are temperate.
From the gods who sit in grandeur
grace comes somehow violent.   [176–83]

The first three lines of this passage are quoted commonly enough as a formulation of Aeschylus' attitude toward human suffering. Certainly, taken in themselves, they reflect the Dionysiac insight that the individual's suffering is validated by the wisdom which results from it, a wisdom which unites all sufferers in a universal "valorization" of the terrors of quotidian existence. Universal wisdom comes through individual suffering. "Still there drips in sleep against the heart/ grief of memory"; and wisdom does not provide an adequate redemption of past griefs. We are reminded here of the blind, exiled monarch of *Oedipus at Colonus*, still raging against the past, against Creon, against his sons, and, in all his wisdom, still suffering. Yes, "from the gods who sit in grandeur/ grace comes somehow violent." He who recognizes this truth is wise; but it would be a broader and deeper wisdom to recognize why the gods supply this violent grace for men. This is a question which cannot be answered in terms of man alone, and its answer requires a knowledge of the gods' motives as well as their actions and particular intentions. It is one thing to know, in the *Eumenides*, that Apollo has commanded Orestes to kill his mother, and now intends to defend him; it is a different thing to know why he has done so. Clytaemestra's crime is not sufficient reason, since it is but one event in a chain of consequence buried in the past amid the seeds of the house of Atreus. If Apollo is merely one agent, one god with motives perhaps different from those of other gods, we must move our attention beyond him to find the final wisdom —the cause of the gods' divisions. Dionysiac wisdom recognizes the contradictions in the ground of Being, but stops there. The individual sufferer demands more, and cannot find it. The vision of anhistorical man is not sufficient for tragic man. It is not enough for tragic man, spiritually dismembered, to recognize his relation to the dismembered Dionysus, though that recognition may be the limit of human wisdom.

The Chorus does not end with the realization that "grace comes somehow violent"; it proceeds to an example of that grace—the bloody warrant for the Argive ships' journey to Troy, the sacrifice of Iphigenia. Agamemnon was granted a particular particle of knowledge about a particular situation: to execute a "war waged for a woman" (225), Helen, it was necessary to sacrifice his daughter. Under "necessity's yoke" (217) he chose "to warp a will now to be stopped at nothing" (221). He acted, seeing the consequence for the war, but not for himself. The Chorus quotes Agamemnon: "May all be well yet" (216); and when it has finished dredging these memories from the depths of the past, it speaks for itself: "All will come clear in the next dawn's sunlight" (254). The Chorus, which has intuited but not explained the contradictions at the ground of human action, now turns to Clytaemestra with something less than Dionysiac wisdom: "Let good fortune follow these things as/ she who is here desires,/ our Apian land's singlehearted protectress" (255–57).

It is evident here and throughout *Agamemnon* that when the Chorus participates in the here and now of the drama, when it engages in dialogue or speaks directly of the action that is passing immediately before it on the stage, it frequently leaves the dark realm of Dionysiac wisdom for the Apollonian illusion that human action is intelligible and that men (and women) are, like the sculptures of Phidias, what they seem to be. The Chorus' dialogue with Cassandra is a crucial instance.

Clytaemestra has just left the stage, having failed to coax Cassandra into the house. She has uttered clear words with a meaning as dark as that of any choral ode: "At the central altarstone/ the flocks are standing, ready for the sacrifice/ we make to this glad day" (1056–57). The altarstone is the bath, and Agamemnon the sacrificial beast. Another will also fall to the sword; she remains outside the house, breaking her silence with a cry to Apollo. The Chorus advises her that Apollo the lucent "has not part in any lamentation" (1079). It recognizes the clear limits of the plastic god, limits which Nietzsche believes essential to his function. But Cassandra claims that Apollo has undone her "once again, and utterly" (1081). She interrupts her lamentation with a question: "What house is this?" (1087). The Chorus answers "The house of the Atreidae. If you understand/not that, I can tell you; and so much at least is true" (1087–88). When Cassandra laments the children who "wail for their own death/and the flesh roasted that their father fed upon" (1096–97), the Chorus informs her that "we want no prophets in this place at all" (1199).

The Chorus' function here is no longer Dionysiac and prophetic; its vision of Apollo is, as it were, Apollonian, denying that there could be an element of Dionysiac darkness in his clear nature. A Chorus which had previously leapt over time and space in its song is now unwilling to move beyond the clear, individual fact—this is "the house of the Atreidae" and "so much at least is true"; it does not pass beyond the limits of this observation. The Dionysiac, prophetic Chorus now wants "no prophets in this place." It has, in short, entered the Apollonian realm of the dialogue, where everything looks "simple, transparent." Cassandra has, in effect, become the Chorus, recalling the dreadful feast which it evoked in its Dionysiac mood. She differs from that seer-Chorus in only one significant respect—her degree of participation in the events which she perceives; she awaits, as an individual, "the sheer edge of the tearing iron" (1149), and so she combines Apollonian individuality with Dionysiac insight, and that insight projects her suffering into a universal.

The chorus-Cassandra sees past, present, and future together, "the slakeless fury in the race" (1117), trapping Agamemnon in a "net of death" (1115). The acts of archaic man "are repeated because they were consecrated in the beginning . . . by gods, ancestors or heroes";[9] and the murder inside the house repeats, with different details and in a different context, the original blood feast of the house of Atreus. The "consecration" here is a terrible one, to be followed by still another—Orestes' murder of his mother. The pro-

tagonists of the *Oresteia* are trapped in the repeated gestures of archaic ontology, which becomes, in this tragedy, a negative rather
than a positive force.

Cassandra's mantic voice remains the stronger in this scene, but
gradually the Chorus is drawn against the edge of Apollonian illusion to deeper perceptions:

> . . . All your speech makes dark my hope.
> And to the heart below trickles the pale drop
> as in the hour of death
> timed to our sunset and the mortal radiance.
> Ruin is near, and swift.   [1120–24]

The Chorus sees, but not enough. It rebels against its own dread:

> From divination what good ever has come to men?
> Art, and multiplication of words
> drifting through tangled evil bring
> terror to them that hear.   [1132–35]

There is a certain truth to its insight; the divinations of Cassandra
do not save her from her death or move the Chorus to action.

A passage follows which illuminates the distinction between the
Dionysiac and its transformation through Apollonian illusion. We
have seen the first in Cassandra's vision of horror; now the Chorus
tells her:

> You are possessed of God, mazed at heart
> to sing your own death
> song, the wild lyric as
> in clamor for Itys, Itys over and over again
> her long life of tears weeping forever grieves
> the brown nightingale.   [1140–45]

The nightingale's song is a pure, balanced, translucent Apollonian
dream image of Cassandra's lamentations. But she sees herself
naked at the edge of the abyss, and cries, "Oh for the nightingale's
pure song and a fate like hers" (1146). Although she rejects the
dream image of her condition, she accepts her Apollonian individuation, realizing that "the pain flooding the song of sorrow is
mine alone" (1137). Yet her individuation exists side by side with
a recognition that her pain sinks to the roots of universal pain,

embracing the conqueror Agamemnon and conquered Troy, both "dragged to uttermost death" (1167).

Cassandra has spoken obscurely, like the mantic Chorus; now she chooses to be clearer, to bring prophecies out, to bring the sun "to burst/at last upon the shining of this agony" (1181–82), Apollo's sun. But her first words are still obscure; she speaks of the presence in the house of "a drunken rout/of ingrown vengeful spirits never to be cast forth" (1189–90)—spirits who will later reveal themselves as the Furies. When she does speak clearly, it is, at first, about herself and the sun-god who has, paradoxically, plunged her into her present darkness: She had promised him children through their union, and broken her word; in return, he has broken the strength of her prophetic word by causing others not to believe in it; and the Chorus does not even understand when she tells it, "you shall look on Agamemnon dead" (1246). The prophecies of Cassandra contribute no more to the characters in the play than do the choral odes. It is as if we were dealing with divided levels of consciousness, both perceived by the audience alone. The protagonists proceed to their several destinies, untaught by the prophetic utterances that surround them. Cassandra is aware of these destinies; the Chorus at the beginning of Agamemnon is not aware of them insofar as they are individual and present on the stage; it only sees (and half understands) the universal patterns which make them inevitable. The Chorus is wise in the general, ignorant in the particular; Cassandra is wise in both, but blocked from effective action. She is the only character in the play who shows that wisdom comes through suffering; Agamemnon does not have time to become wise, and Clytaemestra ends, for the moment, with a shout of triumph. Yet Cassandra shows also, perhaps more fundamentally, that suffering comes through wisdom, and she sings her funeral dirge in pain before the knife falls, this "simple slave who died, a small thing, lightly killed" (1326). Before her death, she utters a prophecy which sees as far as The Libation Bearers, but not beyond:

> . . . We two
> must die, yet die not vengeless by the gods. For there

shall come one to avenge us also, born to slay
his mother, and to wreak death for his father's blood.

[1278–81]

The prophetess' eye sees vengeance in the past, vengeance now, vengeance in the future, set in a pattern of eternal recurrence. The transcendence of this archaic pattern is the one over-arching action of the trilogy. Yet the pattern is not transcended here; and when the bloody work is at last visible, the Chorus cries out against its source:

> alas, the bitter glory
> of a doom that shall never be done with;
> and all through Zeus, Zeus,
> first cause, prime mover.
> For what thing without Zeus is done among mortals?
> What here is without God's blessing?   [1483–88]

Zeus himself is called into question. What are we to say of a god in whom such terrors begin? The question is asked, but not pursued; the Chorus stands poised on the edge of blasphemy, but goes no farther. In a similar fashion, it threatens rebellion against Clytaemestra and Aegisthus, and then backs down. Radical in insight, it is circumspect in action. At the end of the play, Clytaemestra mocks its "howls of impotent rage" (1672), and the Dionysiac Chorus has been reduced to a collection of morally outraged but weak old men.

The Libation Bearers

The homecoming of Orestes, unlike that of Agamemnon, is not lit by a train of torches. Words spoken in *Agamemnon* come to mind; the sorrow of Aegisthus, "driven, a helpless baby in arms, to banishment./Yet I grew up, and justice brought me home again" (1606–7). Justice has brought Orestes home, to another murder; justice, and "the big strength of Apollo's oracle" (269). Apollo has threatened as well as urged him, has spoken of "sicknesses,/ ulcers that ride upon the flesh, and cling, and with/ wild teeth eat away the natural tissue" (279–81). We remember Cassandra's fate, and cannot fail to take the god's threats seriously. If the reasons for his commands are hidden, the cost of disobeying them is very clear indeed.

We have two sets of murders before us—one in *Agamemnon*, one in *The Libation Bearers*. They are seen, however, from different points of view. Clytaemestra and Aegisthus plotted secretly, behind closed doors; an atmosphere of doom prevailed onstage, fed by the insights of the Chorus, leaping from visions of the past to forebodings about the future. The present, shrouded in its antecedents, gradually emerged: first in the cries of Cassandra, finally in the full light of visible fact—the corpses onstage, the murderers revealing their plot and the reasons for it. *The Libation Bearers* proceeds immediately to Orestes' statement of purpose—he prays to Zeus for vengeance for his father's murder. Everything from this moment on will proceed to the fulfillment of that purpose: the reunion with Electra, the prayers for Agamemnon's aid, the enlistment of the Chorus as an accomplice. Everything is visible to us, even the meaning of Clytaemestra's dream. Orestes is the snake she nursed at her breast, the snake who drew blood along with milk. Orestes himself *interprets* the dream, it does not bewilder him as Cassandra's prophecies bewildered the Chorus in *Agamemnon*. The play begins in Apollonian clarity rather than the mantic darkness of the Dionysiac.

The situation, the motives of the protagonists, even the attitude of the Chorus—all these are clear. We do not plunge into darkness until the end, after the murders have been executed. The pattern seems almost a mirror image of what we found in the earlier play; a mirror image which retains certain elements of symmetry: again, two murderers (a man and a woman), two people to be murdered (a woman and a man), and the dead waiting for blood beneath the earth while the gods wait somewhere else.

The Chorus of old men has been replaced by a Chorus of old servingwomen, who, at their first entrance, have just felt "the hard stroke of hands" (22) promised to their counterparts at the end of *Agamemnon*. With this master's stroke, Aeschylus carries the harsh closing rhythm of the first play together with the Apollonian clarity of its closing situation, into *The Libation Bearers*. There is

terror here, but it is visible, and the reasons for it are clear. The
Chorus tells us how "terror, the dream diviner of/ this house,
belled clear" (32–33), and Clytaemestra's dream is no sooner over
than it is correctly interpreted:

> And they who read the dream meanings
> and spoke under guarantee of God
> told how under earth
> dead men held a grudge still
> and smoldered at their murderers.   [37–41]

Agamemnon's ghost haunts his murderers, and

> All the world's waters running in a single drift
> may try to wash blood from the hand
> of the stained man; they only bring new blood
> guilt on.   [72–75]

The disease is visible with its "swarming infection" (70), and the
man who will cure it (or so it seems) is before us—Orestes.

The Chorus' Apollonian clarity of insight is matched by an
equally clear commitment to one side in the plot which is about
to develop, and when Electra asks, "Is there some other we should
bring in on our side?" (114), it tells her to "remember Orestes"
(115). She remembers, and gradually discovers his presence. First,
she sees a strand of hair like hers, lying as an offering on the tomb
of Agamemnon; next, footprints which match her own. The
recognition scene which grows from these discoveries is more than
a moving theatrical set piece; it exhibits a rational movement from
observations to the construction of an hypothesis (Orestes is in
Argos) explaining the observations, to a confirmation of the hypothesis (Orestes presents himself, and places the severed lock
against his hair). The play which will end in madness continues to
proceed in Apollonian clarity.

The Chorus joins Electra and Orestes in prayer to Agamemnon,
prefacing their invocations with this insight: "blood stroke for the
stroke of blood/ shall be paid. Who acts, shall endure. So speaks/
the voice of the age-old wisdom" (312–14). There was an "age-old
wisdom" in the song of the Chorus in *Agamemnon*, but here, for
the first time, it becomes the *basis* of action; murder will proceed

from it as the conclusion proceeds from the major premise of a syllogism, with the murder of Agamemnon the middle term. A seeming clarity pervades everything; but is an "age-old wisdom" enough? The answer does not come through syllogism, since, as the Chorus observes once the prayers are done, "the rest is action" (512), and all wisdom must be tested in its forge.

Orestes acts. It is time for the plot to be executed. While he prepares his disguise, the Chorus sings an ode with Dionysiac insight, and it is, for the moment, more than the accomplice to a murder:

> Numberless, the earth breeds
> dangers, and the sober thought of fear.
> The bending sea's arms swarm
> with bitter, savage beasts.
> Torches blossom to burn along
> the high space between ground and sky.
> Things fly, and things walk the earth.
> Remember too
> the storm and wrath of the whirlwind.   [585–93]

We have left the Apollonian realm of actions with clear consequences, and the realm of syllogism. Who can say if, amid the numberless dangers of the earth, a new murder will bring its hoped-for consequence? "The storm and wrath of the whirlwind" can carry human action where it did not intend to go. Before, there was one doubt: Would the plot of Orestes and Electra succeed? Now the seed of another has been planted: If the plot succeeds, what will be the nature and meaning of its success?

The Chorus does not proceed to the formulation of this question; in its Apollonian mood, with hope still ripe, it tells Orestes' old nurse, Cilissa, to summon Aegisthus without his bodyguard to the presence of a disguised Orestes. Then, the Chorus prays for success, and prays that "the old murder in/ the house breed no more" (805–6); its eye is turned, for a moment, toward the uncertain future.

Aegisthus is dead. Clytaemestra runs from the house, calling for "an ax to kill a man" (889); it will not come in time. She pleads with Orestes and dies, with no deeper tragic insight than this: "You are the snake I gave birth to, and gave the breast" (928). She has not transcended the horizon marked by her personal fate, though the audience sees beyond it.

Still optimistic, the Chorus sings of "our lordships' house/ won free of distress" (942–43), though it confesses to "sorrow even for this pair in their twofold/ downfall" (931–32). Orestes returns to the stage, and, with a clear mind, justifies the deed. It is only now, with the full weight of accomplished action bending over it, that the abyss opens wide before them all. The Chorus sees, no longer abstractly but in fact, "the pitiful work" (1007); and Orestes grieves, in his moment of triumph, "for the thing done, the death, and all our race./ I have won; but my victory is soiled, and has no pride" (1016–17). The insight is unique in one respect. Unlike Agamemnon, who returned in triumph from a war pursued through the sacrifice of his daughter, and unlike Clytaemestra, who exulted over the corpse of her husband, Orestes feels remorse when confronted with his act. He recognizes the defeat implicit in his victory.

Before he leaves, driven by his vision of the still-invisible Furies which Cassandra sensed dwelling in the house, Orestes declares:

> I am a charioteer whose course is wrenched outside
> the track, for I am beaten, my rebellious senses
> bolt with me headlong and the fear against my heart
> is ready for the singing and dance of wrath. But while
> I hold some grip still on my wits, I say publicly
> to my friends: I killed my mother not without some right.

[1022–27]

If his victory is soiled, his crime is not absolute. He affirms the complexity of the content of his actions, its resistance to Apollonian simplicity, the syllogistic clarity with which he and Electra and the Chorus began, believing that the death of Clytaemestra and Aegisthus would cleanse the house of Atreus. His insight is an affirmation of the contradictory ground of human action, which is a projection of the contradictory ground of Being from which Dionysiac insight emerges.

Orestes leaves, hounded by the Furies. Only the Chorus and two dead bodies remain on stage. The Chorus ends the play with a summary of what has gone before, and a question:

> Here on this house of kings the third
> storm has broken, with wind
> from the inward race, and gone its course.
> The children were eaten: there was the first
> affliction, the curse of Thyestes.
> Next came the royal death, when a man
> and lord of Achaean armies went down
> killed in the bath. Third
> is for the savior. He came. Shall I call
> it that, or death?   [1065–74]

The house of Atreus is caught in a net of eternal recurrence. It seemed that the act of its latest member would escape the pattern to find its own unique meaning, that Orestes would, like historical man, "make himself" rather than remake the terrible past. Now it seems that he has failed. The Chorus asks: "Where/ is the end? Where shall the fury of fate/ be stilled to sleep, be done with?" (1074–76). The final chord is unresolved. A play which began in Apollonian clarity ends in Dionysiac turbulence.

The Eumenides

The closing portion of Aeschylus' trilogy begins, significantly, in a physical setting far removed from the house of Atreus. We are outside the sanctuary of Pythian Apollo in Delphi. The disturbed, restless musings of a Watchman prefaced *Agamemnon*, and *The Libation Bearers* began with Orestes, death in his heart, invoking Hermes, lord of the dead; but now we see the Pythia, priestess of Apollo, praying, giving due honor to many gods—old Earth as well as the younger Zeus, Dionysus as well as Apollo. Her harmonious prayer prefigures the harmony of the gods which will emerge at the end of the play.

Yet it is still too early for harmony. The slakeless Furies, whose presence in the house of Atreus was intuited by Cassandra and first made fully visible to Orestes after his vengeance, are now, at last, visible to the audience, "black and utterly/ repulsive" (52–

53), with a "foul ooze" (54) dripping from their eyes. Apollo has, for the moment, put them to sleep within his temple. The god speaks of them as "repulsive maidens . . . with whom no mortal man,/ no god, nor even any beast, will have to do" (68–70). It is now manifest that the conflicts and contradictions that have been displayed in the lives of men have their analogue on the level of the gods. Apollo and the Furies are at odds.

The Chorus of Furies is a Dionysiac embodiment, an aesthetic equivalent to the cruelty of nature and the gods. Unlike the Dionysiac Chorus of which Nietzsche speaks, however, it is committed to action. The Chorus of *Agamemnon* stands, for the greater part of the play, outside the action, an observer of past, present, and future; the Chorus of *The Libation Bearers* aids Orestes and Electra in the execution of their plot, and is therefore more active than its predecessor. The *Eumenides* carries the development a step farther: without the Chorus, there would be no hounding of Orestes, no trial, in fact, no drama.

Here, at last, the Apollonian/Dionysiac duality emerges in its most explicit form, as an opposition between the Dionysiac Chorus and Apollo himself, with Orestes as their ground of conflict. Apollo sees Orestes as historical man, whose unique act must escape from the anhistorical eternal recurrence to which the Chorus condemns him, crying: "Cursed suppliant, he shall feel against his head/ another murderer rising out of the same seed" (176–77). For the Chorus, Orestes is defined within the horizon of archetypal blood murder of the house of Atreus.

The means by which the conflict between Apollo and the Furies is resolved is at least as important as the resolution itself. The ground for mediation is prepared long before the trial which climaxes the play. It is significant that the Furies are, for the first time in the trilogy, visible and audible—embodied. They have emerged from the dark, irrational background of nature into the light of the Apollonian, where dialogue is possible and even the irrational displays itself as rationality. The Chorus justifies itself, and finally gives reasons for hounding Orestes: "We hold we are straight and just. If a man/ can spread his hands and show they are

clean,/ no wrath of ours shall lurk for him" (312–14). It proceeds
syllogistically: all men guilty of kindred blood must be destroyed
by the Furies; Orestes is guilty of kindred blood; therefore Orestes
must be destroyed. The trial will be directed toward the evaluation
of the minor premise; yet it will, in the process, call the major
premise into question.

If the Furies' embodiment is important, so is their willingness to
accept the arbitration of Athene and the decision of a jury of men.
This decision *within* the tragedy is analogous to the pattern of
tragedy as a whole, in which the aesthetic embodiments of Dionysiac perceptions are presented to the judgment of the audience.
The analogy becomes particularly clear when we realize that both
the jury and the audience are composed of Athenian citizens. But
the judgment of Orestes and the judgment of tragedy's Dionysiac
wisdom is not passed from a privileged position; jury and audience
are, perhaps more than they realize, *inside* the action they witness.
Athene's warning rings doubly true for us:

> Yet these, too, have their work. We cannot brush
>   them aside,
> and if this action so runs that they fail to win,
> the venom of their resolution will return
> to infect the soil, and sicken all my land to death.
> Here is dilemma.   [476–80]

Nietzsche sees the cultural equivalent to this dramatic dilemma in
Socrates' rejection of Dionysiac wisdom, an attitude related to the
decline of Greek civilization. The dilemma has an equivalent
breadth of application in Aeschylus' play, where the survival of
Athens is at stake.

The Chorus will argue two points before the jury: the need for
punishing the guilty, the guilt of Orestes. It presents the first point
before a larger jury—the audience—before Athene has returned
with her Athenian citizens:

> There are times when fear is good.
> It must keep its watchful place
> at the heart's controls. There is
> advantage
> in the wisdom won from pain.

> Should the city, should the man
> rear a heart that nowhere goes
> in fear, how shall such a one
> any more respect the right?   [517–25]

The Furies seem to affirm an observation first made by the Chorus in *Agamemnon*—"wisdom/ comes alone through suffering" (177–78). Yet they are themselves a demonstration of that earlier Chorus' observation that "From the gods who sit in grandeur/ grace comes somehow violent" (182–83). "The wisdom won from pain" may be necessary to man; is it sufficient? The Chorus of Furies declares, "I will speak in defence/ of reason" (532–33), but its version of reason leaves man without hope of redemption from distress.

The jurors are assembled, and Orestes' trial begins. We should not be surprised to discover that the opposed arguments of the Furies and Apollo are not always "rational." Their taunts and threats cannot be considered departures from proper trial procedures; these procedures do not, in fact, exist: they are in process of being created. Legal precedents, and human law itself, must emerge from a dialectic in which more than the guilt of Orestes is in question—the *meaning* of guilt, the *standards* of guilt, must be determined. In such a context, the threats of Apollo and the Furies express the opposed claims of fundamental powers in the universe, claims which human justice cannot dare to ignore. Apollo represents one power (perhaps the greatest), Zeus:

> Never, for man, woman, nor city, from my throne
> of prophecy have I spoken a word, except
> that which Zeus, father of Olympians, might command.
> This is justice. Recognize then how great its strength.
> I tell you, follow our father's will. For not even
> the oath that binds you is more strong than Zeus is strong.
> [616–21]

Zeus and his justice are more powerful than the limited bonds of a human jury; yet, as Athene realizes, they are not powerful enough to prevent the Furies from devastating Athens if *their* justice is shunned. Man is impaled by the clashing swords of heaven, the

contradictions in the ground of Being. The Athenians are them-
selves on trial, before two judges with different standards of justice.
This universal trial stands at the heart of the tragedy. The case of
Orestes is, in a sense, merely the path by which it is reached. The
particular arguments for and against Orestes, and the reason for
Athene's final vote, must be understood in this context.

The arguments can be reduced to an affirmation of the opposed
claims of mother right and father right. The Furies declare that
Orestes' matricide was a more sinful deed than Clytaemestra's
murder of her husband, who "was not of blood congenital" (605).
Apollo presents another opinion: "The mother is no parent of that
which is called/ her child, but only nurse of the new-planted seed/
that grows. The parent is he who mounts" (658–60). The ballots
are cast, and Athene gives the reason for what will be her deciding
vote in favor of Orestes: "There is no mother anywhere who gave
me birth,/ and, but for marriage, I am always for the male/ with
all my heart, and strongly on my father's side" (736–38). From a
perspective outside Greek civilization, this decision, and the arguments which precede it, are in danger of seeming trivial, perhaps
even perverse. Orestes' remorse, which seems so important to us, is
never mentioned. Arrowsmith argues that "Orestes kills but first
he hesitates, and the whole world and the fate of mankind hang in
that act of hesitation";[10] but the trial in the *Eumenides* seems to
deny this assertion. The peculiar circumstances of Orestes' act, and
his reaction to it as an individual, have been thrust into the background. The arguments of defense and prosecution could apply to
any matricide whose mother had killed his father.

It is clear, then, that the fate of Orestes and the house of Atreus
are not of primary importance here. But if larger issues are at stake,
why do they seem to hinge on such contingencies as the motherless
birth of Athene?

I suggest that the answer is to be found in the background from
which these seeming contingencies emerge. Behind Apollo and
Athene sits the new ruler of the gods, Zeus, whereas the Furies,
calling to "Darkness of night, our mother" (745), derive from an
older cosmic order formally overthrown but (as the power of the

Furies suggests) not entirely overcome by Zeus. The Chorus springs from what Nietzsche calls "the maternal womb of being," [11] and it affirms its ties with that womb by advancing the cause of mother right. Zeus has cut the umbilical cord which tied him to undifferentiated Being. Significantly, the Furies are manifested as a Chorus, whose members are indistinguishable in appearance, action, and motivation, whereas Apollo and Athene, in spite of their common roots on Olympus, are *individuals,* who differ in all three respects. One god is female, the other male; one mediates the dispute, the other is counsel for the defense; one seeks to placate the Furies, the other heaps scorn upon them. Each has, in addition, individual as well as general reasons for favoring Orestes: Apollo has ordered the death of Clytaemestra by her son's hand; Athene was born without a mother. The fact that Athene is capable of individual prejudice arising from individual circumstances is therefore at least as important as the specific nature of her prejudice. It defines her as a representative of the individuation of the "Apollonian" dispensation of Zeus.

The trial is itself another product of that dispensation. As I suggested earlier, the Furies' willingness to submit Orestes' case to trial is a significant act. A deeply irrational Dionysiac force has emerged into Apollo's light, where it must justify itself dialectically; suddenly, the blood guilt within a family has become a suitable subject for the deliberations of gods and the state. The act of vengeance, whose telos is another act of vengeance (and so on, in eternal recurrence), is replaced by the institution of civilized justice, whose telos is the good of the citizens of a state. Athene makes this clear in her instructions to the jury:

> For Aegeus' population, this forevermore
> shall be the ground where justices deliberate.
> . . . Here the reverence
> of citizens, their fear and kindred do-no-wrong
> shall hold by day and in the blessing of night alike
> all while the people do not muddy their own laws
> with foul infusions. . . .
> I establish this tribunal. It shall be untouched

by money-making, grave but quick to wrath, watchful
to protect those who sleep, a sentry on the land.

[683–706]

In such a context, Orestes' destruction does not follow by necessity
from the act of matricide; rather, both the matricide and the context in which it was committed must be examined in relation to
its effect on the polis. The jury examines the claims of mother
right and father right, casting equal ballots each way, but father
right wins in the end. Are there reasons for this beyond Athene's
family history?

I have already cited Apollo's argument for the prior claim of the
father, a claim which Orestes followed. Behind this is the implica-
tion of Clytaemestra's guilt, a guilt for which, as Orestes observes
(604), the Furies did not pursue her. Clytaemestra murdered a
man not bound to her in blood, but bound by the social convention of marriage. Her crime was, therefore, also a crime against society, a disruption of the order implied by the existence of the
tribunal. In finding Orestes innocent, the tribunal also, in effect,
finds Clytaemestra guilty and affirms a social telos beyond the
limited horizon of blood-relationships. Its decision is in this sense
an inevitable consequence of its existence, in which is implied its
social purpose. The "personal" vote of Athene takes on an objective as well as a subjective content, and the two are coextensive.
Above the new order of the tribunal is the new order of Olympus,
with Zeus at its head, and Athene affirms both orders in her vote.

Yet the Furies cannot be excluded from the polis by a dialectic
with merely social ends; even the Olympians have failed to subdue
them.

The trial has ended. Orestes tells Athene that she has kept his
house alive, and promises eternal friendship to Athens; he leaves
the stage, and with him goes the history of the house of Atreus.
But the play is not over. The house of Man has not been saved;
the Chorus threatens "the vindictive poison/dripping deadly out
of my heart upon the ground" (782–83). The Dionysiac forces of
nature, the ancient law, cannot be subdued by a tribunal of men
or Apollonian gods. Athene offers them a place of their own, "deep

hidden under ground that is yours by right/ where you shall sit on shining chairs beside the hearth/ to accept devotions offered by your citizens" (805–7). Although the Furies refuse at first, the ground has been laid for their acceptance of the offer. In submitting to the trial, they acknowledged the possibility of claims beyond their own, and of a justice which they could not encompass. Dionysiac wisdom recognized something beyond itself—the rationality and individual claims of an Apollonian realm, and the "redeeming illusion" of ideal justice in an ideal polis.

Athene, on the other hand, has acknowledged the need for Dionysiac truth (and its terror) in that polis, which is an institution of civilized men who nevertheless cannot sever their bonds with chaos, with bestiality, with the jubilant celebrations of the satyrs, with everything that transcends the sober individuality and limited, "responsible" actions of the citizen. The Dionysiac Furies are necessary; but how should their power manifest itself? Recall Nietzsche's distinction between the Dionysiac *aesthetic* event and the "terrible witches' brew concocted of lust and cruelty" which lies behind it, and which is related to it as the medicinal drug is related to a "deadly poison." [12] In a similar fashion, Athene posits an *ethical* equivalent to the witches' brew of the Furies:

> in this place that I haunt do not inflict
> your bloodly stimulus to twist the inward hearts
> of young men, raging in a fury not of wine,
> nor, as if plucking the heart from fighting cocks,
> engraft among my citizens that spirit of war
> that turns their battle fury inward on themselves.
>
> [858–63]

The inner Furies of the state must be turned "outward hard against the man/ who has fallen horribly in love with high renown" (864–65), the external enemy. The Furies will put "a spell upon the land" (902), and it is very much like the Dionysiac reveler's vision of a nature flowing with milk and honey:

> Let it come out of the ground, out of the sea's water,
> and from the high air make the waft of gentle gales
> wash over the country in full sunlight, and the seed

and stream of the soil's yield and of the grazing beasts
be strong and never fail our people as time goes,
and make the human seed be kept alive.   [904–9]

By accepting the Furies in their ethical guise, by allowing them
"first fruits/ in offerings for children and the marriage rite" (834–
35), by accepting the fact that nature (and terror, and the recognition of chaos) cannot be isolated from an autonomous polis,
man affirms the harmony of his institutions and himself with the
nature from which both emerged and without which neither could
exist.

If Nietzsche speaks of the marriage of the Apollonian and the
Dionysiac in Greek tragedy, the *Oresteia* presents their union as
something which must be achieved on both the ethical and the
aesthetic levels; it is the outcome of a long, arduous struggle. In
examining the details of that struggle, I have shown that the principles manifest themselves in complex ways that cannot always be
reduced to a contrast between a Dionysiac chorus and an Apollonian dialogue. Yet Nietzsche's major observation remains valid: at
the end Athene, the citizens, and the Furies join for their mar-
riage-processional: "Singing all follow our footsteps" (1047).

What is the version of tragic ontology offered by the *Oresteia*?
Is there a "valorization" of human existence which emerges from
its pattern of pain and redemption? Does the tragic hero affirm his
being by creatively "making himself" within history, the quotidian
realm, or does he draw his being from the imitation of archetypal
patterns of action and suffering?

These questions cannot be answered by separating the tragic
individual from the matrix of action and perception in which he is
embedded, since they deal, in a central way, with his relation to
that matrix. Although both history and the archetype are cultural
concepts, they manifest themselves in different ways in different
works of art. Within Greek culture we have the "culture" of the
Oresteia or of *Oedipus the King*: a particular set of assumptions
about the relation of man to man, to himself, to the gods. If we
examine a culture's total range of artistic, philosophic, and other

documents, we may derive some notion of the assumptions which they share. My (smaller) task has been to find the assumptions of a particular work of tragic art.

Within the world of the trilogy, Orestes, Clytaemestra, and Agamemnon act and suffer. At one point, Agamemnon chooses to walk in triumph over a purple carpet spread before his feet by Clytaemestra; he does not choose the meaning of the act, which he sees as an archetypal gesture of hubris. He does not fall because he has walked on purple; his murder is already planned. Behind it lies the murder of Iphigenia, and a curse on the house of Atreus. His death is not accompanied by what we might call an act of tragic perception on his part, but it does (paradoxically) affirm his being —not as a free agent making his own history, but as a member of a doomed house. The being of Agamemnon is affirmed as being-of-the-Atreidae, and his individuality is absorbed into this archetype. His membership in the house of Atreus is the most important factor in his death, and it is the reason why his executioner is his wife rather than a Trojan or the sea.

Agamemnon is murdered by his wife; Clytaemestra is murdered by her son. Again, the pattern is affirmed. Necessity, anankē, manifests itself as the "eternal recurrence" of a single gesture—the act of blood murder; both Agamemnon and The Libation Bearers affirm an archaic ontology.

This ontology limits the freedom of the individual, who is bounded by the inevitable pattern defined by the archetype. True, he may proceed to the act of blood murder in many ways, but he must proceed to it. To the extent that he is a member of the doomed house of Atreus, it is his telos. But now another distinction emerges. Consider Orestes. His being as a member of his house can be defined at two points—where he murders a blood relation, and where (potentially) he is murdered by one. Otherwise, he is an individual different from, let us say, Clytaemestra, and he feels a remorse at her death which she did not feel at the death of Agamemnon. Furthermore, he kills his mother for a particular reason—she has killed his father. He has, therefore, an individuality which cannot be absorbed into the archetype, an individuality

which either is unimportant ("accident" as opposed to "essence")
or transcends the horizon of the archetype.

The first alternative is clearly rejected by the *Eumenides*, which
rescues Orestes from the archetype by affirming one aspect of his
individuality: his particular reasons for killing Clytaemestra. The
choice is significant. We tend to see the *Oresteia* from a perspective conditioned by two thousand years of Christianity, and Orestes' remorse is significant to us. The individual sinner repents and
is, as an individual, forgiven his sin; this is the Christian pattern.
But Aeschylus was interested in something else—the institution of
civilized justice in a Greek city-state. Orestes' remorse may be important to Orestes, but the structure of the family (a father at its
head, with clear priorities of power) is more important to the polis.

Orestes' case is considered on its individual merits, while the
Furies wish to bind him to the doom prescribed by the archetype.
Yet the case is considered in relation to its impact on the polis
and its universal social consequences. The result is paradoxical: at
the very moment when Orestes' individuality is being affirmed, at
the very moment he escapes from the archetype defined by the
house of Atreus, he is absorbed into a new archetype: the pattern
of civilized justice whose gestures, established here, will be imitated
into all time. Orestes leaves the stage, like historical man, able to
make himself. But the judgment on his case is a paradigm which
will be repeated eternally. Here is the beginning *in illo tempore* of
human law, the movement on a *social* level from chaos to cosmos.
This "new creation" has its divine model in the order represented
by Zeus, who overthrew the older gods and instituted his justice
on Olympus.

But the old dispensation is necessary to the new. Eliade asserts
that "any form whatever, by the mere fact that it exists as such
and endures, necessarily loses vigor and becomes worn; to recover
vigor, it must be reabsorbed into the formless if only for an instant." [13] The same insight seems to inform the end of the *Oresteia*, where the Furies, now transformed into the beneficent Eumenides, join Athene in the devotions of Athens; chaos and cos-

mos, nature and reason, the Dionysiac and the Apollonian, reigning united over Athenian society and its tragic muse.

The vision is a triumphant one, but it contains distressing overtones reminiscent of *Prometheus Bound*. The polis has established its priority over an earlier social unit—the family—with a new promise of order, a new cosmos. But that cosmos, like the one which preceded it, carries the seeds of its own disintegration. Apollo advances the claims of the Olympians with threats of naked power. Here that power is brought to the aid of Orestes and the polis, but it implies, on one level, an unrestrained physis whose implications for man would later be explored by Euripides in tragedies without reconciliation.

· THE GROVE OF THE FURIES ·

Most gentle son of Aegeus! The immortal
Gods alone have neither age nor death!
All other things almighty Time disquiets.
                SOPHOCLES, *Oedipus at Colonus*

AN INTERVAL of more than half a century separates the *Oresteia*
from the last wild dance and cry of Greek tragedy, Euripides'
Bacchae. The distance between these works is enormous; so much
so, in fact, that Nietzsche sees it as a path to the death of tragedy,
with Euripides cast as both poisoner and undertaker, aided by an
apothecary of dialectic—Socrates. According to this view, Sophocles
is a transitional figure, in whose hands the Aeschylean chorus de-
clines in importance, while individual character, "realistically" depicted, begins to take center stage, a tendency brought to completion by Euripides.[1]

The limitations of this interpretation are obvious, particularly in
relation to the *Bacchae*, which in some ways resembles the *Oresteia* more profoundly than does any play by Sophocles: in the
dramatic importance and eloquence of the chorus, for example, or
in the tendency to reduce characters to symbols for opposed forces
(Orestes and Apollo versus the Furies, Pentheus versus Dionysus
and the Bacchae). One way to account for this similarity is to
view the play as a swan song in which Euripides at last affirms the
tragic and religious values which he has denied in his earlier plays.
Here, presumably, would be a "mellowed" artist, turning to tradi-

tional values as T. S. Eliot turned from *The Waste Land* to the bosom of the Church of England. Yet the *Bacchae* is by no means a "mellow" play; its action is transfigured by pain and rage; its Furies, unlike those of the *Eumenides*, have not been tamed. Far more traditional in form than, for example, *Heracles*, it nevertheless presents what may be Euripides' most radical vision of the human condition and the condition of the cosmos.

I cannot account for this vision by accusing Euripides of "esthetic Socratism," declaring, with Nietzsche, that he "set out, as Plato was to do, to show the world the opposite of the 'irrational' poet."[2] It is in Aeschylus, if anywhere, that we are most likely to find a movement from the irrational to reason, from the terror of experience to the resolutions of dialectic, from darkness to light; we may, in fact, argue that this is the entire point of the *Oresteia*. Euripides characteristically presents something quite different: a plunge into the abyss, a revelation of the irrational heart of reason. There is a world of difference and a difference of worlds between Apollo's support for Orestes in the *Eumenides* and Medea's escape in the chariot of the sun-god Helios; it is almost as if the sun had begun to radiate darkness rather than light. The cosmic dislocation implied by this image is not a peculiarity of Euripides' world-view. Beyond the ideal time and space of tragedy lie the quotidian realities of Greek history.

The *Oresteia* was first performed in 458 B.C.; the *Bacchae* was produced after Euripides' death in 406 B.C. Between the two events lies the beginning of the Peloponnesian War in 431 B.C., which was destined to last until two years after Euripides' death.[3] It was a destructive, lacerating war, in which traditional religion and the polis decayed amid the contradictions of chaotic experience, a war to

> Overcome the Empyrean; hurl
> Heaven and Earth out of their places,
> That in the same calamity
> Brother and brother, friend and friend,
> Family and family,
> City and city may contend.[4]

But we do not have to turn to W. B. Yeats' free adaptation of a choral ode from the *Antigone* to find an image of the conflict and its effect on the Greeks; Thucydides is readily at hand:[5]

Practically the whole of the Hellenic world was convulsed, with rival parties in every state—democratic leaders trying to bring in the Athenians, and oligarchs trying to bring in the Spartans. In peacetime there would have been no excuse and no desire for calling them in, but in time of war, . . . it became a natural thing for anyone who wanted a change of government to call in help from outside. . . . In times of peace and prosperity cities and individuals alike follow higher standards, because they are not forced into a situation where they have to do what they do not want to do. But war is a stern teacher; in depriving them of the power of easily satisfying their daily wants, it brings most people's minds down to the level of their actual circumstances.

This abandonment of "higher standards" for time-serving values is exhibited by Neoptolemus in Sophocles' *Philoctetes*: the son of heroic Achilles is tutored in deception by Odysseus so that the Trojan War may be won by the Greeks. To win glory, Neoptolemus must defile himself by a victory over an archer with a festering wound; he must, or so Odysseus lectures, drown both pity and honesty to gain glory.[6] The world of Homer's *Iliad*, an ideal image of a distant conflict fought by men larger than life, has faded before a "necessity" which seems to leave no room for human heroism; indeed, when we are face to face with it, "war is a stern teacher." But Thucydides shows that its lessons are not those of the ordered polis projected at the end of the *Eumenides*:

Revolution broke out in city after city, and in places where the revolutions occurred late the knowledge of what had happened previously in other places caused still new extravagances of revolutionary zeal, expressed by an elaboration in the methods of seizing power and by unheard-of atrocities in revenge.

The barbarity of events is matched by a barbarization of language which is reflected in the tragedies of Euripides:

To fit in with the change of events, words, too, had to change their usual meanings. What used to be described as a thoughtless act of aggression was now regarded as the courage one would expect to find in a party member; to think of the future and wait was merely another way of saying one was a coward; any idea of moderation was just an attempt to disguise one's unmanly character; ability to understand a question from all sides meant that one was totally unfitted for action. Fanatical enthusiasm was the mark of a real man, and to plot against an enemy behind his back was perfectly legitimate self-defence.

Here is a world of extremes, in which Apollonian reason is reduced to the cleverness of the self-serving schemer and Dionysiac emotion submerges the individual in the will of his party rather than an experience of the unity of man with man and man with nature:

Anyone who held violent opinions could always be trusted, and anyone who objected to them became a suspect. To plot successfully was a sign of intelligence, but it was still cleverer to see that a plot was hatching. . . . In short, it was equally praiseworthy to get one's blows in first against someone who was going to do wrong, and to denounce someone who had no intention of doing any wrong at all.

Both the blood ties represented by the Eumenides and the social, legal ties of the polis represented by Athene—principles joined at the end of the *Oresteia*—are destroyed, individually and jointly:

Family relations were a weaker tie than party membership, since party members were more ready to go to any extreme for any reason whatever. These parties were not formed to enjoy the benefits of the established laws, but to acquire power by overthrowing the existing regime; and the members of these parties felt confidence in each other not because of any fellowship in a religious communion, but because they were partners in crime.[7]

Thucydides pictures a Greek world in which the alternatives of human choice are polarized into irreconcilable opposites. Here an Either/Or confronts the individual, and both poles are corrupt, vitiating the polis and those who inhabit it. Sophrosyne is not merely ineffectual; it ruins the individual who practices it: "As for the citizens who held moderate views, they were destroyed by both the extreme parties, either for not taking part in the struggle or in envy at the possibility that they might survive."[8]

It should not surprise us if, confronted by this Either/Or, the difficult synthesis of the Apollonian and the Dionysiac reached at the end of the *Oresteia* begins to disintegrate. Imagine Euripides amid the tumult of his day, looking back—was it only a generation or two, or endless ages ago?—to the final scene of Aeschylus' trilogy. The struggle for order in the *Oresteia* led (so Euripides might reflect) only to the imaginative order of art. If the tragedy enacted in the Theater of Dionysus is a mirror of the spirit of its audience, and of the gods above the stone auditorium, the glass provided by Aeschylus has been warped by the heat of events. It is now a carnival mirror in reverse, transforming perversity and ugliness into glory and harmonious beauty. The actor who plays Orestes stares up through his mask at a spectator whose sword may drip with the blood of parents, sisters, brothers, and thirst for more. The mask of Apollo is struck by Apollo's light. Does the shaft bless the god's image and the words spoken in his behalf, or does it mock them? The light cannot speak. The playwright is confronted by a void, or by chaos. Either the gods are cruel puppetmasters, or man is essentially corrupt, or both. It is possible to see Euripides' plays as attempts to explore these possibilities and the disorder of experience which leads to their postulation.

What shall we say, then, of Sophocles? He lived in the same city as Euripides, spoke from the same stage, and yet wrote what seem vastly different plays. If the polis was dying, were his ears deaf to the death of its values? *Oedipus the King* is generally dated about 427 B.C., four years after the beginning of the Peloponnesian War; *Oedipus at Colonus* was first performed a year or two before the *Bacchae*, near the end of the war.[9] Either Sophocles failed to see what Euripides saw, or he interpreted it differently and wrote plays whose form and attitude reflect that difference. I wish to suggest that the latter choice is the correct one. *Oedipus at Colonus* provides us with an interesting test case. Here, indeed, is a play whose setting and "supra-tragic" resolution seem to imply a world-view more reminiscent of the *Eumenides* than of Thucydides' history. How accurate is the resemblance?

Oedipus at Colonus

In the *Eumenides*, Athene promised the Furies "a place/ of your own, deep hidden under ground that is yours by right" (804–5). Colonus is that place, and it is not far from Athens and the Acropolis where Orestes, a wanderer pursued by the Furies, sought a trial and redemption from his distress. Another wanderer has come now, to Colonus, to the grove of the "sweet children of original Darkness" (106):[10] blind Oedipus, led by a girl. Like Orestes, he carries the weight of kindred blood spilled; unlike Orestes, he also bears the memory of his mother's second bridal bed. And unlike Orestes, he has not been driven by the Furies, but exiled by men. The difference is crucial. It reflects a fundamental difference between the world-views of Sophocles and Aeschylus—but more of that later.

At first we see only the wanderer come to some indeterminate place, one among the thousands of his exile. He observes that "suffering and time,/Vast time, have been instructors in contentment" (6–7). The period of his exile has, in a sense, enabled him to escape temporality, the discontented strivings of men in their quotidian life. This escape will reach its final form in his death and in the meaning of his death.

Oedipus soon learns from a Stranger that the grove, "shady with vines and olive trees and laurel" (17), belongs to the Furies. He remembers Apollo, and the oracle which promised

> A resting place,
> After long years, in the last country, where
> I should find home among the sacred Furies:
> That there I might round out my bitter life,
> Conferring benefit on those who received me,
> A curse on those who have driven me away.   [88–93]

What has been foretold will be fulfilled, as it was fulfilled, most horribly, in *Oedipus the King*. The order of the world remains inscrutable, dealing out pain and joy in hidden ways; but there *is* an order. In a Greece torn by war and revolution, this emerges as an affirmation in the midst of seeming chaos.

Perhaps there is even a value to individual suffering. Oedipus sits

unperturbed "in the inviolate thicket" (127) of Furies whom the
members of the Chorus "tremble to name" (128), and he will go
"without lamentation,/ Illness or suffering" (1663–64) to an end
from which the powerful Theseus must shade his eyes "as if from
something awful,/ Fearful and unendurable to see" (1651–52). In
the end, Oedipus transcends his circumstances; or rather, his individual reaction to them leads him to the circumstance of transcendence. The Orestes of the *Eumenides* is, as I have shown, rescued by a trial which virtually ignores him as an *individual*. He is
crowded from the stage by a larger issue: the institution of civilized
justice in the polis and its recognition of both the Apollonian and
the Dionysiac foundations of society.

This is not the case with Oedipus. His individual character is
delineated with increasingly vivid strokes as the play proceeds. We
are constantly made aware of the difference between him and other
men. At first, he stands separated from the Chorus; unlike them,
he is permitted to stand in the sacred grove. In his suffering and
innocence, he is exalted above the scheming Creon. He is distinguished by the double meaning of his past: an innocence "before
the law—before God" (548), and a pollution which prevents him
from touching Theseus, "a man who has no stain/ Of evil in
him" (1133–34). Theseus was also an exile, but Sophocles makes
it clear that not all exiles are the same. The point is driven home in
Oedipus' reply to the supplications of another exile—his own son,
Polyneices: "When it was you who held/ Throne and authority—
as your brother now/ Holds them in Thebes—you drove me into
exile" (1354–56). Polyneices is repaid—justly—for a consciously
performed crime against his father; Oedipus has suffered for actions beyond his control.

The blind man blesses Athens and curses his sons. He is distinguished from both his friends and his enemies by this double
power. He seems, in fact, an embodiment of that destiny which
ruled him when, in answering the riddle of the Sphinx, he seemed
most like its master. The paradox is complete—or almost complete.
For the power of Oedipus is, unlike that of the gods, tied to his
mortal weakness—his age, his blindness, his dependence on the

good will of Athens. Furthermore, he cannot aid the daughters who aided him, and must tell them, in the moment before his triumphant end, that they will never have more love "from any man than you have had from me" (1618).

The individuality of Oedipus crystallizes at the center of these contradictions, as he justifies his innocence, laments the kidnapping of his daughters by Creon, shrinks from an impulse to kiss Theseus for their return, curses his sons, calmly meets his end. The "supra-tragic" resolution of the *Eumenides* thrusts Orestes (as an individual, complex character) to the side; that of *Oedipus at Colonus* makes it clear that we are witnessing an *individual* redemption, peculiar to Oedipus, inaccessible to any other man. The end of Oedipus will have broader consequences (for both Athens and Thebes), but it cannot, like the trial of a matricide, be repeated with another protagonist at a different time. If Orestes is absorbed into an archetype of civilized justice, Oedipus, in the uniqueness of his destiny and actions, obeys one part of the definition of historical man. This can also be seen in his ability to transform the *meaning* of the past: the Oedipus who once blinded himself in an agony of guilt now declares his innocence, and he is not proven wrong.

In the *Eumenides*, the Apollonian and Dionysiac principles were joined on the level of the polis when the Furies agreed to rule with Athene. Their "marriage" was achieved after a struggle. But now, in the choral ode to Colonus, the principles are firmly united. The Chorus tells us that here, "ever through the shadow goes/ Dionysus reveler,/ Immortal maenads in his train" (678–80), while "Zeus the Father smiles on . . . with sage/ Eyes that forever are awake,/ And Pallas watches with her sea-pale eyes" (704–6). As Oedipus approaches the point where he ceases to be a man and becomes a blessing on the land, as, in a Dionysiac gesture, he merges with its Oneness, his Apollonian individuality becomes more and more distinct. Like the polis, he combines the two principles. His life and actions are intelligible and mysterious; unique, but universal in significance.

Oedipus is himself aware of this universality, and he realizes that only Theseus, the representative of the polis, can be present at his death, which has assumed a more than personal meaning. He therefore remains, in spite of his "historical" individuality, an anhistorical man who has given the stamp of the eternal to quotidian experience. Oedipus' end is glorious, and that glory transfigures, though it does not soften, all his history of pain.

Oedipus' end is, like the grove of the Furies in which it takes place, a still point in the midst of turbulence, a point where the divine impinges on earthly life, and where a man becomes divine. Oedipus approaches this point as the play proceeds. The process is centripetal—aimed at some mythic Center where Apollonian individuality and the Dionysiac universal are affirmed, where Oedipus, in becoming himself, transcends himself. But there is also another, centrifugal process in the play, and it is equally important. The process is evident even in the total rhythm of entrances and exits. Oedipus and Antigone come to the periphery of the Center (the grove). The true Center—the place where he will die—is not reached until the gods and his spirit are ready for it. The grove is a place where the progress of destiny and personality have found, as it were, a geography, less developed but no less significant than Mount Purgatory in Dante's *Commedia*.

A Stranger comes, and warns Oedipus that he must leave the grove; he exits to call the citizens of Colonus. Oedipus withdraws to hide in the grove, but he leaves it again after the entrance of the Chorus, which bids him to come out as far as "that platform there,/ Formed of the natural rock" (192–93); he is not yet ready for the inner recesses of the grove—first, he must justify himself to men and supplicate King Theseus. While they wait for the King, Ismene enters, bringing news of those centrifugal forces which seek to take him to the borders of Thebes. Theseus comes; Oedipus promises that if he is granted access to the grove and the kingly protection this implies, he will grant a blessing to Athens—protection from the sword of Thebes. When Theseus asks, "And how could war arise between these nations?" (606), he answers:

> Most gentle son of Aegeus! The immortal
> Gods alone have neither age nor death!

> All other things almighty Time disquiets.
> Earth wastes away; the body wastes away;
> Faith dies; distrust is born.
> And imperceptibly the spirit changes
> Between a man and his friend, or between two cities.
> For some men soon, for others in later time,
> Their pleasure sickens; or love comes again.   [607–15]

All earthly things, the fortunes and relations of quotidian life, are constantly changed by "almighty Time." Sometimes, of course, the change is for the better: "love comes again." But the emphasis here is on the processes of decay and dissolution, the destruction of the bonds that join man to his life, man to man, city to city. "Faith dies" also, and for Euripides this may be the faith of man in gods as well as the faith of man in man. Behind Oedipus' insight blossom the flowers of blood, fire, and hatred sown by the Peloponnesian War.

The blessing of Oedipus is, like the blessings of Time, double-edged. He promises Athens protection from Thebes in a time of conflict, and is granted asylum for this and other reasons; however, he soon becomes the cause of dissension between the two cities, since Theseus must oppose Creon to protect him. Here the centrifuge is at work. In his movement toward the Center—his transfigured end in the grove—Oedipus shapes the direction of divisions in the external world. It is significant that the scene with Polyneices is the last before thunder and lightning announce his apotheosis in the grove. Oedipus has called a (justified) curse upon his sons, who are destined to die at each other's hands in their struggle for Thebes. Before he leaves, Polyneices asks his sisters for "a grave and what will quiet me" (1409). The *Antigone* has already taught us (and the Greek audience) what this implies. The abyss of "almighty Time" opens wide for others at the very moment when Oedipus is about to transcend it.

Antigone, who has suffered to care for her father, comes to Colonus with him. Later, with Ismene, she is stolen away by Creon's men, then restored by the soldiers of Theseus. But neither sister will reach the Center with Oedipus; unlike Theseus, they will not even be granted the sight of it. At the end of the play they stand lamenting, and the Chorus, pleading that they "must not feed the flames of grief" (1695), cannot quiet them. And they quarrel. Antigone wishes to see "the resting place in the earth" (1726) of her father. Ismene observes, as she will observe later when Antigone wishes to bury a brother, "that is not permitted" (1729). Antigone answers, for the first but not the last time, "Do not rebuke me!" (1730). The geography of the grove is behind them, that of "almighty Time" lies before them. An *individual has achieved blessedness, but what is left for other men?* A charred landscape like that painted by Thucydides, where some will die for their vices (the sons of Oedipus), others for their virtue (Antigone); where some cities will be defeated, and others (Athens) will emerge victorious, at least for a moment. Oedipus' blessing is limited, and Athens will find enemies more terrible than Thebes.

Euripides: The Furies Unleashed

The grove of the Furies established by Aeschylus is still intact in Sophocles, but it seems more an island of peace in the midst of turbulence than the center of civilized values. In Euripides, the olive trees are burnt and the nightingales which inhabited the grove have been exiled, sent out to the cities of men to lament the death of Hippolytus or the fall of Troy. And the Furies range the earth once more in a hundred guises, as if they had never submitted to the yoke of justice forged by Athene.

The Furies of the grove, the Eumenides, represented the full range of Dionysiac powers. They were terrible, yes, but they made the earth yield milk and honey. Oedipus found salvation on their ground. For Euripides, the ground has opened up, and the "terrible witches' brew concocted of lust and cruelty" behind the Dionysiac aesthetic event emerges into the foreground.[11] It should be stressed that the Dionysiac Furies in Aeschylus and Sophocles manifest themselves as a sign of cosmic *order*. Even in the *Eumenides* they represent an old system set against that of Zeus. Their actions are coherent, not arbitrary, and they reflect the orderly (although cruel) operation of a destructive necessity moving through the history of a family. The *destructiveness* of this order, and the limitations that it imposes on the individual and the polis, are chiefly at issue in the *Eumenides*. The contest of two orders—that of Zeus and that of the Furies—results in chaos. The play ends with a resolution of this chaos and a new order, dialectically achieved. It will govern the whole realm of human action.

The new order persists in *Oedipus at Colonus*, but it is no longer all-embracing. Although the contradictions in Oedipus' past are reconciled in the grove of the Furies, there is no resolution for his children or battered Thebes. In the *Eumenides*, an individual (Orestes) is saved, and the polis is rescued from civil war and blood murder. In *Oedipus at Colonus* also, an individual (Oedipus) is saved, and the polis is promised protection from Thebes; but, as I suggested above, Athens is threatened by Thebes because it has permitted the individual to be saved, and Antigone will die because of Oedipus' curse on his sons. The order embracing the world of this play has become tenuous, paradoxical. It is a first step toward what William Arrowsmith calls "the immediate, salient fact of Euripides' theatre," that is, "the assumption of a universe devoid of rational order, or of an order incomprehensible to men." [12] Euripides links the social and political turbulence described by Thucydides to individual man (at one end of the scale of being) and to the cosmic order (at the other end). He does this in plays which reflect and comment on the experience of disorder. It matters little that E. R. Dodds calls Euripides an "irrationalist," while Arrowsmith speaks of his "theatre of ideas"; [13] one author is speaking of the matter examined by the playwright, while the other characterizes the dramatic means by which the matter is examined. A look at two major plays, *Hippolytus* and the *Bacchae*, will indicate both the nature of the experience projected by Euripides and its ontological consequences.

Hippolytus

Arrowsmith observes that "with the sole exception of *Heracles* —Euripides' one attempt to define a new heroism—there is no play which is dominated by the single hero, as in Sophocles' *Oedipus*

or *Ajax*." [14] The observation is certainly correct, but it is important
to observe that essentially the same thing can be said of Aeschylus'
plays. Only in *Prometheus Bound* is there an Aeschylean character
who provides the complete focus of action and suffering normally
found in Sophocles, and Prometheus is atypical—a god rather than
a man. Of the plays I have examined, *Agamemnon* divides its focus between the title figure and Clytaemestra, *The Libation
Bearers* concerns Electra and Orestes, and the *Eumenides*, ostensibly concerned with the fate of Orestes, thrusts him into the
background of a larger duel between Apollo and the Furies.

To discover the nature of Euripides' vision, therefore, we must
move beyond the observation that his plays are not "dominated by
a single hero," to discover how and why he divides his focus on
character. Arrowsmith suggests that "what is striking about the
consistent paired antagonists one finds in Euripides is . . . their
obsessional nature. They function like obsessional fragments of a
whole human soul: Hippolytus as chastity, Phaedra as sexuality." [15]
Hippolytus and Phaedra bear, in short, the same relation to "a
whole human soul" as Apollo and the Dionysiac Furies bear to the
wholeness of the polis in the *Eumenides*, except that the opposed
principles, joined in Aeschylus, engage in an act of mutual destruction in Euripides. This is adequate as a first approximation to the
dramatic facts of *Hippolytus*, but we must move beyond it.

Consider the beginning of the play. A goddess is before us, pre-
senting one of many Euripidean prologues. Aphrodite identifies
herself, assures us of her power, observes that

> Such as worship my power in all humility,
> I exalt in honor.
> But those whose pride is stiff-necked against me
> I lay by the heels.   [6–7]

With Apollonian clarity, she proceeds from this general principle
to a particular instance:

> Hippolytus, son of Theseus by the Amazon,
> pupil of holy Pittheus,
> alone among the folk of this land of Troezen
>   has blasphemed me.   [10–12]

If the general principle is to be obeyed, Hippolytus must be punished. But there is a complicating factor: Hippolytus' failure to worship Aphrodite is tied to his worship for Artemis, and "he is with her continually, this Maiden Goddess, in the greenwood" (17). Will Aphrodite deny the worship of another goddess? She declares:

> I do not grudge him such privileges: why should I?
> But for his sins against me
> I shall punish Hippolytus this day.   [20–23]

The statements here are clear enough; it is merely that, in combination, they do not make sense. Cypris allows Hippolytus his relation with Artemis, but will punish him for his denial of "the bed of love" (13); yet the bed of love is incompatible with service to Artemis. The problem of man's duty to the gods collides with celestial disharmony.

Aphrodite then speaks of Phaedra, who does worship her, who has, in fact, "dedicated a temple to Cypris" (31). If the goddesses are at odds, it should be safer to worship the stronger of the two; but again, this is not the case. Aphrodite outlines her servant's cruel fate, ending with this promise: "Renowned shall Phaedra be in her death, but none the less/ die she must" (47). She is a necessary tool for Aphrodite's revenge, and

> Her suffering does not weigh in the scale so much
> that I should let my enemies go untouched
> escaping payment of that retribution
> that honor demands that I have.   [48–50]

For Aphrodite, the suffering and death of even one of her worshippers weighs lightly "in the scale."

Turning to the epilogue, we discover that Artemis seems to bear the weight of Hippolytus' death more heavily than Cypris bears that of Phaedra, yet even for Artemis there is a limit. She has not, after all, protected Hippolytus:

> This is the settled custom of the Gods:
> No one may fly in the face of another's wish:
> we remain aloof and neutral.   [1328–30]

Yet Hippolytus will be avenged. When he cries, "O, if only men might be a curse to Gods" (1415), Artemis tells him:

> Cypris shall find the angry shafts she hurled
> against you for your piety and innocence
> shall cost her dear.
> I'll wait until she loves a mortal next time,
> and with this hand—with these unerring arrows
> I'll punish him. [1417–21]

A man will be punished for Aphrodite's crime against a man. If men cannot be a curse to the gods, then the gods are effective curses to men. The confrontation of immortal Cypris and Artemis takes place on a human battleground from whose pain the gods withdraw as Artemis withdraws from the presence of the dying Hippolytus, because her "eye must not be polluted by the last/ gaspings for breath" (1438–39).

The position of the gods here is a substantial modification of what we find in the *Iliad*. There too, the gods were immortal; there, although they had favorites, they were safe from death and largely aloof from human suffering. Yet those gods could enter the heat of battle singly or (as in Book XX) in divisions. They acted *alongside* men as well as *through* them. A similar process is visible in the *Oresteia*, where gods and men join in the institution of a civil law which is also a sacred law. In Sophocles, the gods and their motives are hidden, and their plans are revealed in the actions of characters who maintain, in spite of destiny, a human autonomy—witness Oedipus' ability to shape the meaning of his life.

Euripides' Aphrodite tells what will happen to Hippolytus and Phaedra, and she tells *why* it will happen. An immediate mystery is dispelled, but another gapes beneath it. What is the cause of this cause? Human action is no longer mysterious, but divine action has contradictory roots, and both worship and its opposite are dangerous to man. Beyond this, we have the relative calm of Aphrodite and Artemis framing a scene of extreme suffering and death which is somehow incommensurate with their purposes. Either *Hippolytus* is an almost Aristotelian demonstration of the results of failing to worship a god, in which case it must ask why and under what cosmic scheme the worship of two gods should be contradictory; or it shows the disparity between the fact of human suffering and a divine order which can add to that suffering but not comprehend it. Perhaps, at last, the play does both these things.

The prologue and epilogue to the tragedy are not merely ornaments or expository devices: they provide a larger context in which the tragic action must be understood, translating psychology into theology. Conversely, they can be understood only in relation to the tragic action they embrace. I should like to examine that action.

The prologue has ended. Hippolytus and a Chorus of huntsmen enter, singing the praises of Artemis. Hippolytus kneels before the goddess' altar, and speaks of her Meadow:

> No shepherd dares to feed his flock within it:
> no reaper plies a busy scythe within it:
> only the bees in springtime haunt the inviolate Meadow.
> Its gardener is the spirit Reverence who
> refreshes it with water from the river.
> Not those who by instruction have profited
> to learn, but in whose very soul the seed
> of Chastity toward all things alike
> nature has deeply rooted, they alone
> may gather flowers there!   [75–83]

The Meadow is an untouched, natural place like the grove of the Furies in *Oedipus at Colonus*. One basic difference divides them: only the pure have access to the Meadow, whereas the grove is the resting-place of a man burdened with past pollution. The grove can be said to symbolize the double aspect of Dionysiac nature: terror and redemption, the witches' brew of the Furies and the blessings of the Eumenides, original chaos and unity of being. Artemis' Meadow reflects only half of this totality: the order of "inviolate" nature, accessible only to the man who retains his first innocence, unshaken by passion. Later, Phaedra will see the other, violent half of nature:

> Bring me to the mountains! I *will* go to the mountains!
> Among the pine trees where the huntsmen's pack

trails spotted stags and hangs upon their heels.
God, how I long to set the hounds on, shouting!
And poise the Thessalian javelin drawing it back—
here where my fair hair hangs above the ear—
I would hold in my hand a spear with a steel point.
[215–21]

She is thinking of Hippolytus' hunt, but sees it with different eyes; both her vision and that of Hippolytus are valid. The violence of Aphrodite and the maiden calm of Artemis have their equivalents in nature.

Yet the goddesses differ visibly from those equivalents, and also from the human embodiments of the principles they represent. There is no frenzy to the Aphrodite of the prologue, and Artemis, when she appears, maintains the same Apollonian clarity of speech and manner, a clarity which differs from the mysteries of her inviolate Meadow. As characters in the play, both appear in Apollonian embodiments, seemingly simple and transparent. In the play's action, they are revealed as Dionysiac, irrational forces sending Phaedra and Hippolytus to their destruction.

When Hippolytus first comes on stage, he engages in a positive act of worship; before he leaves, a Servant asks him to worship again, at the altar of Aphrodite. He replies: "Men make their choice: one man honors one God,/and one another" (103). Here the choice is freely made; it will not be so with Phaedra. She enters after a Chorus of women sings of her torments, guessing at their source but falling wide of the mark—except for its recognition that there are many springs of sorrow in the world. The Nurse who supports Phaedra takes up the strain in her opening speech:

The life of man entire is misery:
he finds no resting place, no haven from calamity.
But something other dearer still than life
the darkness hides and mist encompasses;
we are proved luckless lovers of this thing
that glitters in the underworld: no man
can tell us of the stuff of it, expounding
what is, and what is not: we know nothing of it.
Idly we drift, on idle stories carried.   [189–97]

Euripides seemed to dispel the awe beyond cognition of Dionysiac
wisdom with his prologue; now, suddenly, we are possessed by it.
Behind the lucent figure of Aphrodite, there is something which
"the darkness hides and mist encompasses." The Nurse is not
speaking from ignorance of the particular cause of Phaedra's condition (though she is, for the moment, ignorant of it), but rather
from knowledge of the *general* cause which links her suffering to
that of all mankind. Men are "luckless lovers" of "something . . .
dearer still than life," and that "something" is a mystery, like Oedipus' end.

The Nurse, who is capable of Dionysiac insight, does not persist
in her vision; faced by Phaedra's torment, she urges Apollonian
moderation, the avoidance of extremes:

> . . . The mixing bowl of friendship,
> the love of one for the other, must be tempered.
> Love must not touch the marrow of the soul.
> . . . So I praise less
> the extreme than temperance in everything.   [252–65]

The ideal for man is sophrosyne, and even Phaedra has the gift of
reason which permits men to perceive it. After she has declared
her passion, Phaedra praises virtue in a long speech which may
seem hypocritical to those who fail to hear these opening lines:

> I think that our lives are worse than the
>   mind's quality
> would warrant. There are many who know virtue.
> We know the good, we apprehend it clearly.
> But we can't bring it to achievement.   [378–81]

The insight embodied in these lines weakens Nietzsche's contention that Euripides is the poet of "esthetic Socratism"; as Dodds
observes, Phaedra "has no Socratic 'illusions of perspective'; she
makes no mistake in her moral arithmetic."[16] The Nurse comes
closer to the truth: "The chaste, they love not vice of their own
will,/but yet they love it" (358–59). If the chaste do not love vice
of their own will, they love it because another "will" is acting
through them. And if personal will is a sign of the individual, possession by another will indicates that the individual has become

absorbed in a force outside himself. It is on this level that Arrow-smith's characterization of "Hippolytus as chastity, Phaedra as sexuality" applies.[17] Both are absorbed in an archetypal passion associated with a divinity, and their individuality is, according to the extent of their absorption, annihilated in the archetype.

In this sense, Phaedra and Hippolytus are embodiments of Dionysiac forces, and their being is absorbed by universals outside themselves. I could go so far as to say that these characters provide the Dionysiac Chorus of Euripides' play. However, the limitations on this statement are both severe and illuminating: the characters are in no sense "above" the action, and they do not join their voices in either a literal or metaphorical sense. It is as if the Chorus of Agamemnon were divided into halves whose lyric insights stood in direct contradiction to each other. Euripides has stripped tragedy of its redeeming illusion to present us with naked truth and its terror. There are contradictions at the ground of Being, and these contradictions, made manifest in men, lead to their destruction. This is the chief wisdom available here, but unlike the wisdom achieved in the Eumenides or Oedipus at Colonus, it offers no redemption for cities and men.

Behind the scene of action there are the gods. The Nurse invokes them when she tempts Phaedra onto the path of destruction:

> Give up your railing. It's only insolent pride
> to wish to be superior to the Gods.
> Endure your love. The Gods have willed it so.
> [474–76]

Opposition is destroying Phaedra, and "endurance" will lead to her death. All the roads of human choice are blocked, or set with traps which cannot be escaped. I am reminded here of the words of the Chorus in Oedipus the King: "When such deeds are held in honour,/why should I honour the Gods in the dance?"[18] Although the question is not, perhaps, central to Sophocles' play, it is a point toward which the action of Hippolytus inevitably moves. This does not indicate that Euripides is an "atheist"—quite the contrary: the gods and what they represent are all too real and malevolent; a universe is split into opposing wheels which grind men between them. Men—not abstractions. Phaedra and Hippolytus are more than the embodiments of Dionysiac forces.

This is particularly true of Phaedra, whose stature as an individual grows from her resistance to the passion which possesses her; Phaedra, who cannot bear to "be discovered/a traitor to my husband and my children" (420–21). The vessel of Aphrodite transcends Aphrodite in complexity and the capacity for suffering. We can turn to the end of the play for a similar lesson. Hippolytus is dying because of his father's curse. When Artemis tells Theseus, "You have sinned indeed, but yet you may win pardon" (1325), she is stating a matter of objective fact; when Hippolytus pronounces forgiveness in his agony, he is engaging in an act of grace inaccessible to the gods, who will carry on their quarrel. It is a short step from this to the final, human heroism of Euripedes' Heracles, who, having killed his wife and children in god-inspired madness, goes out again to face the seas of life "like some little boat." [19]

For a harsher vision, we must turn to Euripides' last play, the *Bacchae*. Here the questions raised by *Hippolytus* assume a new form, outlined in gigantic strokes. Dionysus himself attends the tragic dance, with the Bacchic Chorus in his train.

The Bacchae

The play begins, like *Hippolytus*, with a prologue spoken by a god. If Aphrodite felt slighted by Hippolytus, Dionysus and his birth have been slandered by his mother's sisters and the young king Pentheus, and even his status as a god is in question. Dionysus will prove to "every man in Thebes that I am god/indeed" (48–49), and he will prove his deity as Aphrodite proves hers, through an act of destruction.

Dionysus reveals himself first of all in his Apollonian individuality: as one god affirming his claims among others. Unlike Aphrodite, he will not withdraw from the stage and work his will through the heart of a Phaedra: he will be both visibly present and manifest in his effects.

The Chorus of this play is quite literally Dionysiac; it is com-

posed of the possessed followers of the god, the "attending chorus" of which Nietzsche speaks.[20] At the end of the prologue, it
bursts upon the stage with a long and ecstatic song of worship un-
precedented in Euripides. The god's history unfolds in its song, and
then a vision of the union of man with primal nature:

> O Thebes, nurse of Semele,
> crown your hair with ivy!
> Grow green with bryony!
> Redden with berries! O city,
> with boughs of oak and fir,
> come dance the dance of god!   [105–11]

This Dionysiac oneness with nature embraces its savagery as well as
its grace. The Chorus speaks of Dionysus:

> He drops to the earth from the running packs.
> He wears the holy fawn-skin. He hunts the wild
>   goat and kills it.
> He delights in the raw flesh.   [135–38]

And yet, "With milk the earth flows! It flows with wine!/ It runs
with the nectar of bees!" (142–43), and the blessing and the curse
of Dionysus are inseparable.

Like Phaedra in *Hippolytus*, the Bacchae wish to run *"to the
mountain! to the mountain!"* (165); they do not seek the inviolate
meadow of Artemis, though there may be a special kind of purity
in their worship. Unlike Phaedra, whose yearning is tied to the
hunt and the hunter Hippolytus, the Bacchae exult in nature for
its own sake. Images of nature on the mountain dominate the
choric songs in the *Bacchae* as emphatically as the inescapable past
dominates those of *Agamemnon*. Aeschylus' play is enveloped in
the history of the house of Atreus and the expedition to Troy;
Euripides surrounds his with streams, with trees, with leaves, with
the lowing of cattle and the lion's thunder.

In his analysis of the symbols of archaic societies, Eliade lists
two occurrences of the "symbolism of the center": "1. The Sacred
Mountain—where heaven and earth meet—is situated at the center
of the world. 2. Every temple or palace . . . is a Sacred Mountain,
thus becoming a Center."[21] At the end of the *Oresteia*, the Acropo-

lis becomes just such a Center—a meeting ground of the gods and men, where the issues that divide them are resolved, and where tribunals will maintain the life of the polis through its laws. In *Oedipus the King*, the grove of the Furies is the Center, the point at which the destiny of the gods fuses with the will of a single man in whom mortality and divinity are miraculously joined.

The *Bacchae* presents us with two Centers. One—the palace of Pentheus—is present to our eyes. The other—the mountain of the Bacchae—is present to our imaginations, its glories sung by the Chorus, the actions which transpire there reported by messengers breathless with awe or terror. Yet the Centers are not harmonious reflections of each other; indeed, the palace of the state and nature's mountain are at war.

In their first song, the Bacchae describe the union of ecstatic man with nature and his god, Dionysus, on the Sacred Mountain. They fill the stage with their exultation and images of a potent nature. When they have ended, the first representative of the civilized Center, the palace, appears. He is, significantly, a doddering blind man, the prophet Teiresias. He is followed by old Cadmus, "who built the towers of our Thebes" (172). Both lean on a thyrsus and are dressed in Dionysiac costume; their goal is the mountain, and worship—to "tread the dance, tossing our white heads/in the dances of god" (183–84). Teiresias justifies their journey:

> We do not trifle with divinity.
> No, we are the heirs of customs and traditions
> hallowed by age and handed down to us
> by our fathers. No quibbling logic can topple them,
> whatever subtleties this clever age invents.
> [200–203]

The affirmation of the "traditional" nature of Dionysus-worship seems at odds with the god's own account of his recent coming to Thebes; furthermore, he is the son of Semele, who was the daughter of the still-living Cadmus. In what sense is his worship a tradition "hallowed by age"? Perhaps we must recognize a distinction between the individual god Dionysus and the Dionysiac principle, whose irrational roots may be traced back to (for example) the Furies, or to the Void, Earth, and Eros, primitive gods who stand at the beginning of Hesiod's theogony. In any case, we see the "historical" and the "archetypal" god side by side, as it were; the first is the son of Semele and a new god in Thebes; the second has his origins *in illo tempore,* "the mythical time of the beginning of things."[22]

Teiresias has affirmed the existence of an archaic Dionysus who manifests himself in tradition. His speech is barely completed when Pentheus bursts upon the scene, protesting against the novelty of

> mock ecstasies among the thickets on the mountain,
> dancing in honor of the latest divinity,
> a certain Dionysus, whoever he may be!   [218–20]

Pentheus, as king, is the source of power in the civilized Center, and he flaunts his power with threats against the Bacchae and their leader,

> . . . one of those charlatan magicians,
> with long yellow curls smelling of perfumes,
> with flushed cheeks and the spells of Aphrodite
> in his eyes.   [234–37]

The king sees Dionysus as the mask for Aphrodite, and, like Hippolytus, he rejects the goddess.

William Arrowsmith sees the god and the king as antagonists who "embody the principles of conflicting ideas; Pentheus as *nomos,* Dionysus as *physis.*" Elsewhere he defines physis as "nature," nomos as "custom, tradition, and law."[23] But Teiresias speaks of Dionysus in terms of "customs" and "traditions," and the Chorus will pick up this strain later. How can Dionysus be alternately nomos and physis? Dodds throws some valuable light on the puzzle:

Nomos could stand for the Conglomerate, conceived as the inherited burden of irrational custom; or it could stand for an arbitrary rule consciously imposed by certain classes in their own interest; or it could stand for a rational system of State law, the achievement which distinguished Greeks from barbarians. Similarly

Physis could represent an unwritten, unconditionally valid "natural law," against the particularism of local custom; or it could represent the "natural rights" of the individual, against the arbitrary requirements of the State; and this in turn could pass—as always happens when rights are asserted without a corresponding recognition of duties—into a pure anarchic immoralism, the "natural right of the stronger" as expounded by the Athenians in the Melian Dialogue.[24]

Dionysus is seen as both "the inherited burden of irrational custom" (nomos) and "natural law" (physis) against the "arbitrary requirements of the State" as exhibited through its ruler, Pentheus. Pentheus himself is more than a representative of nomos; there are elements of the doctrine of the "natural right of the stronger" (physis) in his obsessive threats against Dionysus and the Bacchae. What nomos can he be said to obey when he threatens to hunt his mother Agave from the mountain like an animal? Arrowsmith's equation (Pentheus/Dionysus equals nomos/physis) does not seem to work here. It is equally tempting to set up another equation: Pentheus/Dionysus equals Apollonian/Dionysiac. But Pentheus' Apollonian individuality is not matched by an Apollonian avoidance of extremes. There is, in fact, a strong Dionysiac current of irrationality running beneath the king's actions, and this becomes increasingly clear (and increasingly disastrous) as the play proceeds.

The *Bacchae* reveals the full nature of Dionysus gradually, as Sophocles' *Oedipus the King* loosens, knot by knot, the tangled skein of the past. Every man has his image of the god, and no image is complete. When he speaks to Pentheus, the Teiresias who earlier suggested a Dionysus-worship "hallowed by age" (202) declares that "this god whom you ridicule shall someday have/ enormous power and prestige throughout Hellas" (272–73) and argues for present submission to a future power. Before the entrance of the old men, the Chorus sang of the birth of Dionysus:

> Zeus it was who saved his son; . . .
> in his thigh as in a womb,
> concealed his son from Hera's eyes.   [95–99]

Even this event is presented to us in two versions. Teiresias tells
how Zeus,

> . . . Breaking off
> a tiny fragment of that ether which surrounds the
>   world,
> . . . molded from it a dummy Dionysus.
> This he showed to Hera, but with time men garbled
> the word and said that Dionysus had been sewed
> into the thigh of Zeus.   [291–96]

Here we have an instance of the seer turned linguistic scholar, and,
perhaps, an instance of the "rationalistic method" of whose use
Nietzsche accuses Euripides.[25] Yet we must distinguish between
the words of Teiresias and the deeds of Dionysus, whose irrational
potency affirms most clearly an irrational origin, a birth shrouded
in the mysteries revealed by the Chorus.

Like Teiresias, Cadmus has his reasons to accept the god, and
offers Pentheus this advice:

> Even if this Dionysus is no god,
> as you assert, persuade yourself that he is.
> The fiction is a noble one, for Semele will seem
> to be the mother of a god, and this confers
> no small distinction on our family.   [333–37]

Cadmus is speaking of the historical Dionysus, whose Center is the
palace rather than the mountain, the Dionysus born at a definite
point in time and related to a particular human family. Such a
Dionysus can, presumably, be dealt with rationally and in relation
to a reasonable end—for example, the family's prestige.

The arguments of Cadmus and Teiresias fail to stir Pentheus,
except to greater rage. Like Dionysus, he does not argue, he acts:

> Go, someone, this instant,
> to the place where this prophet prophesies.
> Pry it up with crowbars, heave it over,
> upside down; demolish everything you see.   [346–49]

But "the place where this prophet prophesies" is, in the final analysis, the Sacred Mountain, and no man can "heave it over," as a
god will later overturn the palace. Pentheus is as absolute and as

savage in his will as Dionysus, but he lacks effective power. The
Chorus sings of the king when he has left the stage:

> what passes for wisdom is not;
> unwise are those who aspire,
> who outrange the limits of man.   [395–97]

And it tells us of the benefits granted by Dionysus, and the piety
proper to man:

> The deity, the son of Zeus,
> in feast, in festival, delights.
> He loves the goddess Peace,
> generous of good,
> preserver of the young.
> To rich and poor he gives
> the simple gift of wine,
> the gladness of the grape.
> But him who scoffs he hates,
> and him who mocks his life,
> the happiness of those
> for whom the day is blessed
> but doubly blessed the night;
> whose simple wisdom shuns the thoughts
> of proud, uncommon men and all
> their god-encroaching dreams.   [417–29]

This is an Apollonian vision of Dionysus, like the Apollonian vision
of the Furies represented by the Eumenides; here the god seems
lucent, his gifts transparent, his worshippers cloaked in a sophrosyne
that avoids challenging the gods. The most positive aspects of nomos
and physis are joined in this perspective. Here, as in the *Eumenides*,
we see a ground where nature, tradition, and law meet. The Chorus
assures us that "what the common people do,/the things that simple men believe,/I too believe and do" (430–32), and the union
with one's fellow is also a union with divinity. The perspective here
is that of the Sacred Mountain, but that Mountain is now the City
of Man as well, hallowed by tradition and guided by sacred law.

But this vision is a lyric interlude between the angry exit of the
"proud, uncommon" Pentheus and his entrance with Dionysus in
chains. It will be proved incomplete, like the formulations of

Teiresias and Cadmus. For the moment, Dionysus is mild and peaceful. The attendant tells Pentheus:

> We captured the quarry you sent us out to catch.
> But our prey here was tame: refused to run
> or hide, held out his hands as willing
>   as you please . . .
> making no objection when we roped his hands
> and marched him here. It made me feel ashamed.
>
> [435–41]

Here indeed is a mild and moderate god, almost Christ-like, surrendering himself to the soldiers. Yet appearances will prove deceptive. Dionysus has freed the women chained in the dungeon, and the Attendant reports that "the chains on their legs snapped apart/ by themselves" (447–48). The god who performed this miracle will not allow himself to be subjected to the equivalent of a crucifixion; he has other plans.

Furthermore, this god of "simple men" answers the questions of Pentheus with confident irony and a subtle indirection:

PENTHEUS. Tell me the benefits
    that those who know your mysteries enjoy.
DIONYSUS. I am forbidden to say. But they are worth knowing.
PENTHEUS. Your answers are designed to make me curious.

[472–75]

It is only a step from here to Pentheus' female disguise and his death. But there is more at issue than the power and weakness of a king:

PENTHEUS. Have you introduced your rites
    in other cities too? Or is Thebes the first?
DIONYSUS. Foreigners everywhere now dance for Dionysus.
PENTHEUS. They are more ignorant than Greeks.
DIONYSUS.   In this matter
    they are not. Customs differ.   [480–84]

At this point, we may be vividly reminded of an unusual fact: in this Greek tragedy with a Greek setting, the Chorus which occupies the stage is not native to the place. The Choruses of *Agamemnon* and *Oedipus at Colonus* were saturated with the values and a sense of the value of their Greek cities; but the home of the

Bacchae, ostensibly Asia, is more basically the Sacred Mountain where they join in the dances of their god, and its geographical location is not of central importance. The *Eumenides* and *Oedipus at Colonus* end with a blessing on Athens, but the Thebes of the Bacchae is less important, and its representatives (Pentheus, Cadmus, Teiresias, Agave, and the Maenads) are seen primarily in relation to a god who has come from foreign parts to conquer a city. The centrifugal effect evident on one level of action in *Oedipus at Colonus* here reaches its final form; it is no longer possible to see the city-state as the center of civilized values, or to see its laws as the resolution of human and divine conflicts implied by the climax of the *Oresteia*. The Greek revolutions described by Thucydides, the wars of brother against brother and class against class, have split the fabric of Greek civilization. When Pentheus declares that foreigners "are more ignorant than Greeks," he is stirring the ashes of Pericles' funeral oration. The king's hubris is the hubris of Greece, based on a power which will fail when confronted with a greater power.

Like Greece, Pentheus is divided against himself, and will go blindly to his end. Dionysus tells him:

> You do not know
> the limits of your strength. You do not know
> what you do. You do not know who you are.   [505–7]

The king answers, "I am Pentheus, the son of Echion and Agave" (508); yet even his physical identity will be obscured in a wig and women's robes.

For the moment, his threats seem effective, and the Chorus fears him, "Inhuman, a rabid beast,/a giant in wildness raging" (542). Dionysus is brought to the dungeon of the palace. Now the human Center is shaken; "the great stones/gape and crack!" (591–92), the palace falls, and the Chorus announces theophany:

> Down, Maenads,
> fall to the ground in awe! He walks
> among the ruins he has made!
> He has brought the high house low!
> He comes, our god, the son of Zeus!   [599–603]

The act has been accomplished, Dionysus declares, "with ease" (614). The god is cheerful. He tells the Chorus: "I shall not be touched to rage./ Wise men know constraint: our passions are controlled" (640–41).

Pentheus appears. He has been shaken by the escape of "that stranger, that man/ I clapped in irons" (642–43), but he has not been moved to contemplate the meaning of the disaster. It is clear by now that he, like the Maenads, is possessed, but his possession is a blindness opposed to their vision. He seems as self-absorbed as the Bacchae are absorbed in their god, a radicalization of Apollonian individuality without the harmonious moderation of Apollonian man. Even the first Messenger's story cannot stir him from his obsession.

The Messenger begins with a lyrical account of the Dionysiac state; he has seen the Maenads on the mountain,

> some resting on boughs of fir, others sleeping
> where they fell, here and there among the oak leaves—
> but all modestly and soberly, not, as you think,
> drunk with wine, nor wandering, led astray
> by the music of the flute, to hunt their Aphrodite
> through the woods. [684–89]

What seemed Pentheus' chief complaint against the followers of Dionysus has been refuted; and yet, characteristically, he is blind to the refutation. The Messenger proceeds to describe the harmony of the Maenads with nature after they awake:

> . . . Breasts swollen with milk,
> new mothers who had left their babies behind at home
> nestled gazelles and young wolves in their arms,
> suckling them. Then they crowned their hair with leaves,
> ivy and oak and flowering bryony. One woman
> struck her thyrsus against a rock and a fountain
> of cool water came bubbling up. [698–705]

This harmony is invaded by cowherds and shepherds struck with awe but anxious to please their king. Violence is met by violence; the shepherds are routed. But the Maenads' anger also encompasses the beasts with which they had been in harmony:

> Unarmed, they swooped down upon the herds of cattle

grazing there on the green of the meadow. And then
you could have seen a single woman with bare hands
tear a fat calf, still bellowing with fright,
in two, while others clawed the heifers to pieces.

[735–39]

Their violence spreads to the villages before it ends. Two conclusions are obvious here: First, it is unwise to interfere with those
who are possessed by Dionysus, and the commands of kings cannot prevail against them. Second, the followers of the god are
capable of miracles of *both* harmony and destruction.

A different king, confronted by these facts, might decide that
the worship of Dionysus leads to extremes dangerous to the state,
and conclude that it should be suppressed (if possible) or accepted
with moderation within the framework of law, as the Furies are
accepted by Athens in the *Eumenides*. But Pentheus is viewing
an extreme state from an extremist standpoint, promising: "I shall
make a great slaughter in the woods of Cithaeron" (798). If opposites are joined in the Maenads, we should not be surprised to
find them joined also in Pentheus.

Quite suddenly, the king who hates the Maenads and their
leader admits that he "would pay a great sum" (812) to see their
mountain revels. Indeed, he will pay a great sum. The obsession to
destroy has been replaced by an obsessive curiosity, and both will
lead to his death. The two are linked by his individuality; the ob-
sessions of Pentheus, unlike those of the Bacchae, do not proceed
from an annihilation of individuality in the service of divinity. Yet
they will proceed *toward* an annihilation of individuality. Dionysus
suggests the first step: Pentheus must dress himself in women's
clothes to view the Maenads with safety. Pentheus himself described Dionysus' "long yellow curls smelling of perfumes" (235)
with contempt; now this human relative of the god will look very
much like the god who, with a grotesque intimacy, will help him
dress.

A choral song fills the space between the exit of the god and his
return with Pentheus. It includes this passage:

Beyond the old beliefs,

> no thought, no act shall go.
> Small, small is the cost
> to believe in this:
> whatever is god is strong;
> whatever long time has sanctioned,
> that is a law forever;
> the law tradition makes
> is the law of nature.   [891–96]

The essential identity of nomos and physis is being posited here. If the duel between Pentheus and Dionysus seemed in part a conflict between the two principles, we must now see it in different terms. The recognition of the unity of nomos and physis is, perhaps, a Dionysiac wisdom; but we are about to view the Dionysiac act.

The god returns from the palace, and Pentheus follows him—or the man who was Pentheus. Dionysus flatters him: "Why,/you look exactly like one of the daughters of Cadmus" (916–17). He has been transformed—in appearance—from a king to one of the women he sought to hunt and destroy. But the transformation goes beyond appearances; Pentheus has tasted the god's wine or been enchanted by him (which is the same thing), and his vision is intoxicated:

> I seem to see two suns blazing in the heavens.
> And now two Thebes, two cities, and each
> with seven gates. And you—you are a bull
> who walks before me there.   [918–21]

Dionysus assures him, "It is the god you see./ . . . You see what you could not/when you were blind" (922-25). He does not deceive Pentheus on this point; intoxication has made the king's sight more, not less accurate, although he still lacks foresight.

Dionysus spends a few moments arranging the king's curls and dress. The Pentheus who once expressed his kingliness through threats and brute force is now entirely submissive to Dionysus, and the obsessive individual has so lost his individuality that even his sex is transformed. Pentheus has been "dancing for joy" (930) in the palace, like a Maenad; his costume is merely the outer sign of an inner state.

Pentheus senses within himself the power of the Dionysiac state:

> PENTHEUS. Could I lift Cithaeron up, do you think?
> Shoulder the cliffs, Bacchae and all?
> DIONYSUS.   If you wanted.
> Your mind was once unsound, but now you think
> as sane men do.   [945–48]

The god's answer is doubly ironic. We have already heard of the superhuman power of the Maenads; the thoughts of Pentheus would perhaps be "sane" thoughts for them. The same complexity informs Dionysus' last speech to the king:

> You are an extraordinary young man, and you go
> to an extraordinary experience. You shall win
> a glory towering to heaven and usurping
> god's.   [971–73]

The promise will be fulfilled. Like the mythic Dionysus, dressed in curls like his, Pentheus will be dismembered, and the pieces of his body gathered together.

Nietzsche speaks of the tragic hero as a Dionysiac mask, an Apollonian embodiment "in which Dionysus assumes objective shape." He speaks also of the *suffering* of Dionysus, and of "dismemberment—the truly Dionysiac suffering" which symbolizes the evil of individuation.[26] Pentheus is perhaps the clearest instance of Nietzsche's tragic hero in Greek drama. He takes on the appearance of Dionysus; he is intoxicated with the god; he will suffer a dismemberment which displays the evil inherent in his individual will. Yet Dionysus himself is on stage, and this modifies the meaning of Pentheus' death. This god, like the Olympians in *Hippolytus*, cannot suffer.

What shall we say of his followers, the Bacchic Chorus? Nietzsche makes this observation: "Notwithstanding its subordination to the god, the chorus remains the highest expression of nature, and, like nature, utters in its enthusiasm oracular words of wisdom. Being compassionate as well as wise, it proclaims a truth that issues from the heart of the world."[27] Yes, nature sings through the Chorus, and the Bacchae are wise. But are they compassionate, in the sense that the Choruses of *Agamemnon* and *Colonus* are compassionate? The Bacchae will have no gentle words for Agave when she returns from the mountain with her prize; they will be silent, except to affirm the justice of their god's revenge. We learn the reason when the second Messenger comes with his news:

MESSENGER. . . . Pentheus, the son of Echion, is dead.
CORYPHAEUS. All hail to Bromius! Our god is a great god!
MESSENGER. What is this you say, women? You dare to rejoice
   at these disasters which destroy this house?
CORYPHAEUS. I am no Greek. I hail my god
   in my own way. No longer need I
   shrink with fear of prison.
MESSENGER. If you suppose this city is so short of men—
CORYPHAEUS. Dionysus, Dionysus, not Thebes,
   has power over me.
MESSENGER. Your feelings might be forgiven, then. But this,
   this exultation in disaster—it is not right.

                     [1030–40]

The Bacchae, like the Furies in the *Eumenides*, are alien to the city within whose walls they find themselves. The society which it represents is, for them, accidental, whereas their god is necessary. Aeschylus' Furies at last find a place in the life of the polis, but the Bacchae will move on with their leader to conquer new lands. Who, then, will be left in Thebes? Agave? Cadmus? Citizens we have never seen, left without a king? The abyss which opens in the last scene is social as well as individual in its repercussions. Set in tiers above the stage of the Theater of Dionysus, an audience sits amid the echoes of the Peloponnesian War. Furies range among them, or Bacchae with Dionysiac rage but without Dionysiac compassion or wisdom. The ceremonial blood of art stains the actors, but real blood stains the auditorium, and the Greek world is the true Theater of Dionysus, playing a drama without redemption.

For the moment, however, our attention is on the stage. Agave has returned. The Chorus preludes her entrance with a song of praise:

      Hail, Bacchae! Hail, women of Thebes!
      Your victory is fair, fair the prize,
         this famous prize of grief!

> Glorious the game! To fold your child
> in your arms, streaming with his blood!
>
> [1160–64]

Here we have Dionysiac terror without Dionysiac compassion, fear without pity. The Chorus will have ironic words for Agave, but it will not project her suffering into the universal. A proposition about divinity has been proved: Pentheus is dead, therefore Dionysus is indeed a living god.

Agave will suffer horribly, having denied the divinity of Dionysus; but Cadmus, politic and accommodating, will suffer also. In *Hippolytus*, both Hippolytus (who denies Aphrodite) and Phaedra (who has built a temple to her) are destroyed. The *Bacchae* places us in a similar moral universe, made even more terrible by the physical presence of the destructive god and his alien Chorus.

After drunkenness and sleep comes the moment of waking. Agave discovers that the "lion's head" (1278) she is holding is the head of her son. She is standing where Oedipus stood when the Shepherd had answered his final question, but with a different stance. Oedipus discovered a truth about the tragic order of the world and of his life; what has Agave discovered? The divinity of Dionysus? Her possession and that of the Maenads was sufficient proof of it. Perhaps she has discovered the difference between gods and men. If Pentheus has enacted the dismemberment of Dionysus, she cannot knit his pieces together again, completing his imitation of the god. Mortals are not resurrected. Furthermore, we have observed Agave possessed, a Maenad, godlike in her powers, but not godlike in her vision. The power of Dionysus without Apollo's light has caused her to destroy her son.

Agave passes from Dionysiac intoxication to a clear, Apollonian vision of her act. It is important to realize that this shift in perspective, this movement from self-transcendence to self, to the *principium individuationis*, is an important concomitant of her humanity. It is not until she is restored to her individual identity that Agave recognizes the identity of the "lion" she has killed. Here she ceases to be a follower of the god, saturated with divinity, and becomes a human mother. Without this transformation, Agave

could not suffer, and the "lion" would remain a lion in her eyes, a
glorious prize of the hunt.

In Sophocles' *Oedipus the King* we are, at first, strongly aware of
Oedipus, an individual with a clear will pursuing the murderer of
Laius. Gradually, we pass from the Apollonian clarity of the visible
action to a perception of the Dionysiac forces at work above the
narrow skene. Tragic perception in *Oedipus* is an "explosive" process, moving outward from Thebes' visible center to the vast and
inscrutable order of the gods. In the *Bacchae*, a god reveals both
himself and his plans for Thebes in advance, and his Chorus reveals, even in its first song, the order of the god's natural domain,
the Sacred Mountain of the Bacchae. Here tragic perception seems
to be an implosive process, moving from Dionysiac visions to an
awareness of the suffering of men on the visible stage. The reticence of the Dionysiac Chorus after the entrance of Agave empha-
sizes this change. We are face to face with the pain of individuation, unmediated by Dionysiac perception. The Chorus does not
meditate upon the *universal* meaning of the action which has
passed; instead, Dionysus, the visible Apollonian mask of the Dionysiac principle, calmly and lucidly reveals the *individual* suffering
which remains for Agave and Cadmus.

Oedipus raised the golden brooches above his eyes, and in that
act affirmed the universal order which destroyed him, transforming
what could have been unmediated suffering into tragic exaltation.
When he left, a maimed man, the Chorus of a purified Thebes remained on the stage. But Greece and its tragic mirror have changed
for Euripides. These are Agave's final words:

> Lead me, guides, where my sisters wait,
> poor sisters of my exile. Let me go
> where I shall never see Cithaeron more,
> where that accursed hill may not see me,
> where I shall find no trace of thyrsus!
> That I leave to other Bacchae.   [1381–86]

Agave does not in any sense embrace the divine order which has
destroyed her, and a weary despair rather than tragic exaltation
pervades the final minutes of Euripides' last play. Compelled to

acknowledge the divinity of Dionysus, which she once rejected, Agave now rejects the validity of Dionysiac experience in her own life; that she will "leave to other Bacchae." Banished like Oedipus, she does not leave a band of purified citizens behind her, but rather the god and an alien, Asiatic Chorus. Thebes has not been purged but conquered, and the alien army will move on to other victories. A sword falls across the future as well as the present; Cadmus is doomed by Dionysus "to live a stranger among barbarian peoples, doomed/to lead against Hellas a motley foreign army" (1355–56) and lead "spearsmen against the tombs and shrines of Hellas" (1359), desecrating what is most sacred.

The disintegration of the polis described in Thucydides' history has been given a divine context by Euripides. The *Bacchae* suggests that the powers which rule the world are, like individual men, flawed or corrupt, and at the same time capable of far more harm than their mortal counterparts. We have seen the arrogance of Pentheus, but Agave is brought before our eyes only to suffer, and that suffering seems, in the final analysis, more characteristic of mankind. It is the chain that binds Pentheus, Agave, and Cadmus in the *Bacchae*, the common bond of Hippolytus and Phaedra in *Hippolytus*. Outside the circle of lamentation, the gods smile and act, and a sword is raised whose edge cannot be turned by any man-made shield.

The Death of the Polis

The preceding analysis suggests a definite shift away from the tragic "valorization" of human existence found in Aeschylus, a shift whose relation to Greek historical change seems too close to be merely accidental.

In the last chapter, I explored the archaic ontology inherent in the *Oresteia*, where Orestes escapes the archetypal pattern of blood murders of the house of Atreus only to have his actions absorbed into another archetype—the pattern of civilized justice, whose gestures are destined to be repeated forever. Here the meaning of the tragic hero's existence is tied to the polis, whose order rests on a balance between Apollonian and Dionysiac forces, the

Olympian gods and the Furies. The Acropolis becomes a "Sacred Mountain—where heaven and earth meet,"[28] a Center where divine and human conflicts are resolved and the redemption of an individual (Orestes) becomes also the redemption of the polis.

The Center in *Oedipus at Colonus* is the grove of the Furies, from which the terrible daughters of Night exercise a beneficent influence over Athens. At this meeting place of heaven and earth, Oedipus reaches the final valorization of his existence: he is accepted, with the full weight of his tragic past, by the gods. Unlike Orestes, he is redeemed as a complex, suffering *individual* rather than a test case of father right versus mother right. At the moment of his death, he transcends this individuality to become a blessing on Athens—but the act remains individual and unique; unlike the trial of Orestes, it does not establish a paradigm for future generations. The blessing which Oedipus offers Athens—protection from Thebes—is *particular*, and it can control only one fraction of the attritions of "almighty Time" (609), whose quotidian abyss confronts Antigone and Ismene at the end of the tragedy. The valorization of Oedipus' *individual* life does not necessarily imply a general tragic valorization of all human existence. We have moved a step away from an archaic ontology.

In *Hippolytus* there are two Centers, two meeting places of the divine and the earthly—Hippolytus and Phaedra. Although the "inviolate Meadow" (78) of Artemis and the mountains of Phaedra's erotic imagination stand in the background, the warring goddesses of this play manifest themselves above all through their mortal instruments, who are at once individuals and the representatives of archetypal passions. Here, as in the *Eumenides*, there is a confrontation of gods. In Aeschylus' play, however, the conflict is mediated by human and divine judges; as a result, the warring Centers merge, and the tragic individual, Orestes, is redeemed in an act which also redeems the polis. In *Hippolytus*, the polis seems almost superfluous, Aphrodite and Artemis are not reconciled, and the tragic individuals are destroyed. However, Phaedra has struggled against her passion, and Hippolytus forgives his father in a gesture which is not embraced by any definition of "chastity"; and both *suffer*, a fact emphasized by the calm presence of the goddesses. We may say that Phaedra (for example) draws her ontological status from the imitation of the archetype of passionate love, the primal gesture of Aphrodite. On the other hand, we may assert that she affirms her being in the act of *resisting* Aphrodite; then the suffering which grows from this resistance is a sign of the ontic value which she has assigned to her existence.

According to this latter view, *Hippolytus* would represent a step away from archaic ontology, toward a vision of historical man, who *is* insofar as he *makes himself*. Finally, however, Phaedra is less able to make herself and the meaning of her life than is the protagonist of *Oedipus at Colonus*. Perhaps the archaic ontology affirmed by *Hippolytus* differs from that achieved in the *Oresteia* chiefly in its irrationality and its grim insistence on destruction. Instead of the eternal recurrence of the act of civilized justice, we are faced with the eternal recurrence of a duel between eros and chastity. The passage from chaos to cosmos so central to Aeschylus' trilogy is missing here; the Furies of the earlier play are reconciled to the Olympians and mortal men, but Aphrodite and Artemis will continue their quarrel, on a field littered with human lives.

The *Bacchae* provides an even more radical version of archaic ontology. Pentheus dies dressed as a Maenad, with the long yellow curls of Dionysus on his head; his mother mistakes him for a young lion, a beast of prey like Dionysus who "delights in the raw flesh" (138), and, like the Dionysus of myth, he is torn limb from limb. He has "imitated" the god, however unwillingly. Agave herself acts as an inspired instrument of Dionysus, a Maenad full of the god's power for miracles both glorious and terrible. Yet this absorption in divinity is ultimately destructive. The human characters cannot complete the transition from chaos to cosmos. Pentheus does not rise, like Dionysus, from his pieces, and Agave, confronted with her son's death at her hands, rejects her fusion with divinity to go where she "shall find no trace of thyrsus" (1385).

The gods are not at war with each other here, but Dionysus is at war with men. When the Bacchae declare that "Beyond the old beliefs,/ no thought, no act shall go" (891–92), they are like the

Furies in the *Eumenides* speaking of "old rights" (847), and Dionysus is himself like a new version of the Dionysiac Furies, with no Apollo or Athene present to balance his destructive power. The Apollonian and Dionysiac Centers of the *Oresteia* at last merge on the human and holy ground of the Acropolis, but the *Bacchae* offers two Centers which do not achieve unity—the palace of Pentheus and the Sacred Mountain of Dionysus. Dionysus conquers, and the vanquished are buried in the ground or go into exile. The "defeat" of Aeschylus' Furies was followed by their acceptance by men, but the rule of Dionysus is seen, at the very moment of its triumph, as intolerable to mortals. The audience must either leave the stage with Agave and Cadmus or merge with the exultant, inhuman silence of the Bacchic Chorus. Euripides' play gives us archaic ontology with a vengeance, the opposite of any redemptive "valorization" of human existence. In this sense, it prepares the ground for an escape from divine archetypes and a movement toward historical man, freely creating his life in a quotidian realm emptied of divinity.

The death of archaic man suggested by the *Bacchae* is accompanied by the decay of the positive and redemptive values inherent in the Apollonian and Dionysiac principles. Pentheus is characterized by Apollonian individuality, but not by the Apollonian avoidance of extremes. His individuality is, in fact, asserted in most extreme terms. Dodds speaks of "*koros*—the complacency of the man who has done too well—which in turn generates *hubris*, arrogance in word or deed or thought." [29] The hubris of Pentheus is exceptional, perhaps unique in Greek drama; the less reason the king has to display koros, the more absolute his hubris, and even the destruction of his palace moves him only to increased rage against Dionysus.

A similar process is evident in relation to the second principle. In spite of the Chorus' references to a nature flowing with milk and honey, Dionysus reveals himself most fully in that terrible witches' brew of cruelty which the Dionysiac attempts to transcend. We have come a long way from the redemptive Dionysiac powers in the grove of the Furies, and the joyous shattering of the

principium individuationis is less a merging with mystical Oneness than a tool for the shattering of human individuals; both the
false Maenad Pentheus and the true Maenad Agave fall beneath
its blows. Dionysiac wisdom is no longer awe before the inscrutable, but horror before the intolerable.

In Euripides' last play, the god who presided over the Theater
of Dionysus may have emerged at last to announce, in person, the
death of both Apollonian and Dionysiac culture. He faced an audience steeped in the final cruelties of the Peloponnesian War,
Maenads of the polis who would wake (like Agave) to the horror
of sons and brothers slain by their own hands, and Hellas dismembered with no hope of resurrection. In the passages I quoted earlier
from Thucydides, we can witness the reduction of the Apollonian
and the Dionysiac to the brutality of unrestrained individualism
and the fanaticism of party. If Aeschylus celebrated the birth of
the polis, in whose context men and opposed principles could be
reconciled, Euripedes celebrated its death and the end of recon-
ciliations. Aristotle is more than justified in calling him "the most
tragic of the poets";[30] in Euripides we can discover the tragedy of
Greek culture, separated by historical experience from its "Divine
Comedy," the *Oresteia* of Aeschylus.

·THE TRAGIC UNIVERSE OF *KING LEAR*·

It is by all means to be believed, because it is absurd.

TERTULLIAN, *De Carne Christi*

TWO millennia separate Euripides and Shakespeare—two thousand years in which the tragic art slept while empires, philosophies, and religions rose and fell. The chief accomplishments of Roman drama were in the realm of comedy, and the medieval mysteries offered the universal comedy of a Christian world, Dante's world. Did this world supply the framework of values from which Shakespearean tragedy emerged in all its harsh splendor?

The question has been actively debated. Sylvan Barnet, for example, suggests the limitations of a Christian approach to Shakespeare:

Shakespeare, it is argued, was a Christian, and his audience thought in Christian terms. Now as St. Paul realized, the heart of Christianity is the resurrection, for if Christ is not risen, faith is a foolish hope, and death is not succeeded by life. The Christian pattern moves from weakness to strength, from death to life, from sin to bliss. Its form is therefore comic, and Dante writes a *Commedia* because he knows that a tragedy begins quietly and ends in horror, while a comedy begins harshly but concludes happily.[1]

Barnet's reasoning is persuasive, and it does manage to account, in part, for the "comic" movement evident in the medieval cycles. If there is a redemptive pattern in Shakespearean tragedy, it is, certainly, of a different order. Yet there are also undeniable similarities between the tragedies and medieval drama. Both differ from Greek tragedy in their scenic vastness, the use of comedy in serious actions, the multiplicity and development of secondary characters.

The analogy which suggests itself here is an old one: Shakespearean tragedy is constructed like a Gothic cathedral. And, as H. D. F. Kitto observes,

The unity of the cathedral is such that it could include, besides formal decorations, representations in stone, wood or glass of prophets, saints, martyrs, kings; and these it could combine harmoniously with carved foliage, animals, birds, fishes. . . . All things are the creation of God; all things therefore have their own unique value, and all things combine to proclaim the glory of God.[2]

Kitto notes "the complete absorption, the loving care, with which the medieval mason will carve a flower or a dog. Each separate thing has a double value: it is part of the whole, and it is itself—a unique creation existing in its own right." Here, indeed, is a notion of order which justifies the multiplicity of minor characters and subordinate incidents in Shakespeare, and their vitality—since "only if they are real and vivid will they fulfill their true function, which is to suggest that the central tragic action is part of the great stream of human life."[3] To restate the matter: the ontic value of a person, an animal, an object lies both in its unique individuality and its relation to the whole, and the *principium individuationis* is affirmed together with its opposite.

The general significance of this process becomes clear in Erich Auerbach's study of *figura* in *Scenes from the Drama of European Literature*. John Dennis Hurrell, in an essay which explores the significance of Auerbach's work for the study of medieval drama, tells us how "he traces the meaning of the word from its first appearance in Terence's *Eunuchus* (317) where it means simply 'plastic form,' to its development into a concept of artistic form as a whole which is a mirror of the form God has given to his world."[4]

Auerbach discusses the "figural interpretation" of the Bible from its beginnings in Tertullian through St. Augustine, to its central position in medieval thought. He explains its meaning in these words:

Figural interpretation establishes a connection between two events or persons, the first of which signifies not only itself but also the second, while the second encompasses or fulfills the first. The two poles of the figure are separate in time, but both, being real events or figures, are within time, within the stream of historical life. Only the understanding of the two persons or events is a spiritual act, but this spiritual act deals with concrete events whether past, present, or future, and not with concepts or abstractions; these are quite secondary, since promise and fulfillment are real historical events, which have either happened in the incarnation of the Word, or will happen in the second coming.[5]

For example:

Figural interpretation changed the Old Testament from a book of laws and a history of the people of Israel into a series of figures of Christ and the Redemption, such as we find later in the procession of prophets in the medieval theater and in the cyclic representations of medieval sculpture.[6]

As this example indicates, the concreteness and historicity of figural interpretation, although greater than that of abstract allegory, is by no means absolute. Seen in its perspective,

earthly life is thoroughly real, . . . but . . . with all its reality it is only *umbra* and *figura* of the authentic, future, ultimate, the real reality that will unveil and preserve the *figura*. In this way the individual earthly event is . . . viewed primarily in immediate vertical connection with a divine order which encompasses it, which on some future day will itself be concrete reality. . . . But this reality is not only future; it is always present in the eye of God and in the other world.[7]

The historical unfolding of events, although real and measurable on a temporal scale, has its ultimate reference in God's eternal order, a reality *outside* time.

It is clear from even these few passages that the *figura* is profoundly relevant to a consideration of the position of historical and anhistorical habits of thought in the Middle Ages. Eliade approaches the same problem by way of its Hebrew origins. The linear progression of history, he declares, was real for the Hebrews, who succeeded in transcending the cyclic vision of archaic man. The prophets conceive of a God who revealed his will through events. Therefore historical facts "become 'situations' of man in respect to God, and as such they acquire a religious value that nothing had previously been able to confer on them." The Hebrews "were the first to discover the meaning of history as the epiphany of God," a conception adopted and elaborated upon by Christianity. We no longer have the archetypal gestures *in illo tempore* of archaic gods and heroes; "Moses receives the Law at a certain place and at a certain date."[8] In this scheme, the terrors of history, the disasters which afflict the Chosen People are, although irreversible, not meaningless—they are revelations of God's will in history. Suffering is not absurd.

Although the Old Testament grants meaning to the irreversible historical event, its

Messianic beliefs in a final regeneration of the world themselves also indicate an antihistoric attitude. Since he can no longer ignore or periodically abolish history, the Hebrew tolerates it in the hope that it will finally end, at some more or less distant future moment. . . . History is thus abolished, not through consciousness of living an eternal present (coincidence with the atemporal instant of the revelation of archetypes), nor by means of a periodically repeated ritual (for example, the rites for the beginning of the year)—it is abolished in the future. Periodic regeneration of the Creation is replaced by a single regeneration that will take place in an *in illo tempore* to come. But the will to put a final and definitive end to history is itself still an antihistoric attitude.[9]

The Hebrew's attitude toward history is, in short, double-edged: it combines a recognition of the significance of historical events with a vision in which history is finally to be abolished. This is the double attitude at the basis of the *figura*, which accepts the concrete validity of historical events and at the same time refuses them a "definitive self-sufficient reality," since their reference is to a divine order "which on some future day will itself be concrete reality."[10]

For Christianity in particular, that "future day" is already present, as Auerbach observes, "in transcendence," and the histori-

cal event is "in immediate vertical connection with a divine order." [11] Eliade agrees with this interpretation, and notes its significance for the individual:

In Christianity . . . the evangelical tradition itself implies that
βασίλεια τοῦ θεοῦ [the Kingdom of God] is already present
"among" (ἐντός) those who believe, and that hence the *illud
tempus* is eternally of the present and accessible to anyone, at any
moment, through *metanoia*. Since what is involved is a religious
experience wholly different from the traditional experience, since
what is involved is faith, Christianity translates the periodic regeneration of the world into a regeneration of the human individual.[12]

Here we are face to face with the individual "history" of salvation,
whose crucial significance for the Christian experience is evident
in St. Paul's conversion or in the pages of the *Confessions* of St.
Augustine. Eliade continues:

For him who shares in this eternal *nunc* of the reign of God, history ceases as totally as it does for the man of the archaic cultures,
who abolishes it periodically. Consequently, for the Christian too,
history can be regenerated, by and through each individual be-
liever, even before the Saviour's second coming, when it will utterly cease for all Creation.[13]

The medieval Christian is, in the final analysis, involved in an escape from the linear, temporal progression of history—and this
links him to archaic man. Furthermore, Christianity establishes
an archetype for man in the imitation of Christ, although the
archetype is established in time (the historical life of Christ)
rather than *in illo tempore*.

Clearly, historical man is not yet the central figure of Western
culture. Even the archaic rituals of eternal recurrence have their
equivalent here, in the Christian liturgical year and in that concrete reactualization of the birth, death, and resurrection of Christ
which lies at the heart of the medieval mystery plays. The Wakefield cycle is an instructive example. Scenes from the life of Christ
dominate the extensive middle portion of the cycle, which begins
with the Creation and ends with the Last Judgment. Yet the Son
is mentioned as early as the fifth line of the first play, and he
dominates the cycle even when he is not "historically" present in a

given play.[14] The linear temporal progression of the cycle has reference to a reality which, although it was revealed in time, lies finally in God's transcendent reality *outside* time.

Medieval drama, then, has its final reference in this reality. From its perspective, Christ is "present" on the stage as he is "present" in the rituals of each liturgical year and in the souls of individual Christians. From the same anhistorical perspective, medieval English peasants may be "present" at the "time" of Christ's nativity, as they are in the *Second Shepherd's Play*. Thus a drama enacted in historical sequence affirms a world-view which transcends history.

Shakespearean tragedy is also permeated with anachronisms, comic scenes, departures from the classical unities. However, the life of Christ does not occupy center stage in his theater, and Christian ideas frequently manifest themselves in highly unorthodox ways. Thus Hamlet's father comes from purgatorial fires to demand a very unchristian act of vengeance against his murderer, and Othello atones for the murder of Desdemona with a suicide which should, in a Christian context, damn him. Shakespeare seems to have assimilated some elements of the medieval worldview while rejecting others; the significance of both choices is a central problem of this chapter.

I shall consider a play which is universally acknowledged as a crucial instance of Shakespeare's tragic vision. Although the gods of the Hellenic world are dead, the terrible affirmations of Dionysiac insight are with us again, and Apollo's measured light breaks on the flood of the world, marking the stricken features of suffering men. The passage of time has produced a new drama, but man and his passage on the earth remain, in spite of Christianity, pervaded with mystery and paradox.

King Lear: Act I

Consider, for a moment, the analogy between Elizabethan drama and the Gothic cathedral. The details of a cathedral's architecture are not of equal importance, though all contribute to the whole. But the central portal *is* important: small and somewhat two-dimensional when compared with the echoing chambers of light and darkness within, it is nevertheless a necessary transition from the street and marketplace to nave and vault, from quotidian experience to a vision transcending it.

In *King Lear*, we approach the entrance obliquely, as it were— along the street fronting the cathedral. We see, beside the door, three figures sculptured in stone: Gloucester, Edmund, and Kent. In a moment, our eyes will turn to a scene ordered symmetrically on the tympanum above the portal: King Lear in the center, surrounded by his daughters and their men. The doors are about to swing open.

The play begins simply enough. Gloucester mentions "the division of the kingdom" (I, i, 3),[15] and the equal qualities of the Dukes of Albany and Cornwall. Kent then asks about the identity of the silent Edmund:

GLOU. . . . I have so often blushed to acknowledge him that now I am brazed to it. . . . Do you smell a fault?
KENT. I cannot wish the fault undone, the issue of it being so proper.
GLOU. But I have a son, sir, by order of law, some year elder than this, who yet is no dearer in my account.   [I, i, 9–19]

Symmetry and moderation pervade the opening moments of the play. Albany and Cornwall weigh equally in the balance, and the bastard is loved no less than the legitimate son. Gloucester has learned to live with his "fault," and, after all, its issue was "proper." Sin is viewed in the Apollonian light of reason and moderation, and its fruits are illusions as lucent as Edmund's shape, his "dimensions . . . as well compact . . . /As honest madam's issue" (I, ii, 7–9).

When King Lear enters, he affirms what seems (given his time of life) a reasonable plan: "To shake all cares and business from our age,/Conferring them on younger strengths while we/Unburdened crawl toward death" (I, i, 39–41). Lear's plan has been called foolish by commentators aware of its consequences, but we cannot accurately judge it in relation to what follows unless we first consider it in its *immediate* context. Here Lear at least *seems* wise—aware of his mortality, aware of the needs of the state, anxious "to publish/ Our daughters' several dowers, that future strife/ May be prevented now" (I, i, 43–45).

Lear's plan is eminently *rational*, as is his appeal to his daughters to publicly declare the measure of their love for him. It assumes what amounts to a quantitative, almost mathematical connection between seeming and being, rhetoric and substance. Recall how, earlier in the scene, Edmund was declared (in effect) no bastard, since he seemed none.

These actions assume a lucid, Apollonian universe, one in which appearance is wedded to essence. Lear's first error is as much a defect in reason as an error in reasoning. This is equally clear in his first exchange with Cordelia:

> LEAR. . . . what can you say to draw
> A third more opulent than your sisters? Speak.
> COR. Nothing, my lord.
> LEAR. Nothing?
> COR. Nothing.
> LEAR. Nothing will come of nothing.   [I, i, 90–95]

As the play will gradually reveal, this "nothing" must be understood in a more general sense than the immediate context might seem to warrant. In Lear's first, rational universe, "Nothing will come of nothing" bears the weight of a mathematical truth. Yet the Christian world was created from nothing by God, who transcends all merely quantitative truths, and Lear, in the ostensibly pagan universe of the play, will grow through the perception of his own nothingness and the nothingness of man. It is as if the insight of the Chorus in the *Agamemnon* that "wisdom/ comes alone through suffering"[16] has been transformed into the realization that being comes alone through nothingness. Such an insight is paradoxical, like the Christian vision of freedom in man's surrender to God, and it establishes an important link between the tragic universe of *Lear* and the Middle Ages.

The order of reason in this scene proves to be illusory. Regan and Goneril are immoderate in their protestations of love for their father, while Cordelia's reasonable recognition that she must grant half her love to her husband is greeted by Lear's immoderate rage.

Nature and the gods are called to witness his rejection of a daughter: "the sacred radiance of the sun,/ The mysteries of Hecate and the night" (I, i, 116–17). Lear is in the realm of extreme action and passion, the Dionysiac realm; but he lacks Dionysiac wisdom. He will now attempt to divide power from kingship, while remaining a king. He tells Cornwall and Albany:

> I do invest you jointly with my power,
> Preëminence, and all the large effects
> That troop with majesty.
>   . . . Only we shall retain
> The name, and all th' additions to a king.
> [I, i, 138–44]

If Lear's individuality is tied to his kingship, which distinguishes him from other men, he has severed his *principium individuationis* from reality, and it is destined to be shattered by events.

The scene ends with Regan and Goneril on stage, plotting "i' the heat" (I, i, 336) against their father. Scene ii begins with Edmund's soliloquy; the bastard desires his brother's land and plans to deceive his father. Here the second of *Lear's* parallel plots is launched. Shakespeare's handling of these plots brings to mind the medieval *figura*, except that here the "figures" are not separated by vast stretches of time, but rather spatially and hierarchically. The daughters of a King and the son of an Earl are engaged in the initial stages of an act of betrayal—the first in Lear's palace, the second in Gloucester's castle. Each act retains its concrete individuality, and is saturated in its own set of unique circumstances. Lear's legitimate daughters (two of them) are contrasted with Gloucester's illegitimate son; Lear has divided his kingdom, Gloucester has not. Although the two sets of events are distinct, their dramatic juxtaposition and obvious similarities support their figural relation, while pointing us beyond the particular circumstances involved in each to a general order that embraces them. Here, for example, we are made aware of a world in which children (bastard or legitimate) may betray a father. The particular act becomes saturated with a universal significance.

This indicates that plot, in Shakespeare, can assume at least one of the functions of the Greek chorus. It helps to project particular action and passion to a vision of the contradictions at the Dionysiac ground of Being. The Chorus of *Agamemnon* binds past and present, man and nature, king and polis in a vision of tragic reality which both embraces and transcends them. Lear's double plot is one of several means by which Shakespeare accomplishes the same thing. Scene ii reveals another—the perception, by individual characters, of parallels between natural and human events. Gloucester, who thinks himself abused by his son Edgar, speaks:

These late eclipses in the sun and moon portend no good to us. Though the wisdom of nature can reason it thus and thus, yet nature finds itself scourged by the sequent effects. Love cools, friendship falls off, brothers divide. In cities, mutinies; in countries, discord; in palaces, treason; and the bond cracked 'twixt son and father. [I, ii, 102–8]

The last sentence indicates Gloucester's particular error (he suspects Edgar), but as a general observation it can be accurately applied to the present situation (Edmund *is* his son) and extended beyond it—to a prediction of the division between Lear and his daughters.

What are we to make, then, of Edmund's comment after his father has left the stage?

This is the excellent foppery of the world, that, when we are sick in fortune, often the surfeits of our own behavior, we make guilty of our disasters the sun, the moon, and stars; as if we were villains on necessity; fools by heavenly compulsion; knaves, thieves, and treachers by spherical predominance. [I, ii, 116–21]

Edmund's comments revolve around the conflict between interpretations of human action in terms of free will and of necessity, and he chooses the first of these. The play itself, however, indicates that things are by no means so simple. Perhaps human action is not determined by "the sun, the moon, and stars," but nature acts *as if* it bears some coherent relation to the realm of human action—the storm on the heath is just one significant example. The meaning of this relation cannot be found in any one speech, but is unfolded as the play progresses, through what we might call the montage of particular utterances and actions.

The Fool occupies a unique position in the drama. Although capable of suffering, he is in a sense, by virtue of his profession, set apart from the principal action. Like the Greek chorus, he speaks bitter truths from a privileged vantage point, and is the repository of traditional wisdom. His "identity," like that of the chorus, is qualified by his function, and although the disguised Kent assumes a name, the Fool has no name but Fool. Unlike the chorus, however, he is not always on stage. He attends Lear; yet we do not hear of him until I, iv, and hear no more of him after III, vi. This suggests that he is only one path to Dionysiac insight; yet he becomes an important one from the moment of his appearance.

I have neglected to mention that the Fool, unlike the Greek chorus, is a vehicle of comic perceptions. If we regard this fact from the perspective of medieval drama, it is not at all surprising. The laughter in the mysteries is an expression of one aspect of a comprehensive world-picture; an aspect which cannot be excluded from the Creation. Analogously, we might say that the comic in Lear provides a vision of those aspects of quotidian experience which are not embraced by the tragic action, a vision, as it were, of other, contrary currents in life's turbulent ebb and flow. Yet this fails to account for our sense that the jests of the Fool in King Lear are an integral part of the tragic current, part, in fact, of the play's specifically tragic vision.

The Fool begins by chiding the disguised Kent, who is a fool "for taking one's part that's out of favor" (I, iv, 97). He knows how the world turns; he gives practical advice. Yet his pragmatism is only a part of what he has to offer in the way of wisdom, and it hides a paradox. "If thou follow him, thou must needs wear my coxcomb" (I, iv, 101–2); but the Fool himself will follow his master out of fashion, even into the eye of the storm.

He reminds us of the opening scene, and Cordelia's dower:

FOOL. . . . Can you make no use of nothing, nuncle?
LEAR. Why, no, boy. Nothing can be made out of nothing.

FOOL. [*To Kent*] Prithee tell him, so much the rent of his land
   comes to. He will not believe a fool.   [I, iv, 128–33]

The Lear of the first scene knew that "nothing will come of nothing" (I, i, 95), yet failed to apply it to his own situation. The Fool
supplies the logical link between a general principle and its particular application. He also shows us the principle in a context
which amplifies its meaning.

LEAR. Dost thou call me fool, boy?
FOOL. All thy other titles thou hast given away; that thou wast born
   with.   [I, iv, 146–48]

Lear is confronted with his nothingness, though he does not yet
comprehend it; yet the Fool has begun to prepare him for that
moment when he will turn to a half-naked Edgar and ask, "Is man
no more than this?" (III, iv, 107–8).

    The Aeschylean Chorus projects its universal Dionysiac insights
through elevated diction and imagery: "Their cry of war went
shrill from the heart,/as eagles stricken in agony/for young perished."[17] Contrast the Fool:

FOOL. . . . Nuncle, give me an egg, and I'll give thee two crowns.
LEAR. What two crowns shall they be?
FOOL. Why, after I have cut the egg i' the middle and eat up the
   meat, the two crowns of the egg. When thou clovest thy crown
   i' the middle and gavest away both parts, thou borest thine ass
   on thy back o'er the dirt. Thou hadst little wit in thy bald crown
   when thou gavest thy golden one away.   [I, iv, 153–61]

The Fool speaks in prose (as in this instance) or bantering verse;
his images are generally reductive rather than expansive (a crown
is reduced to an eggshell); and the paradigm of his traditional wisdom is the Aesopian fable rather than myth. Furthermore, he explains his simile and its applicability to Lear's situation. The
Aeschylean Chorus takes a particular event—Thyestes' feast, the
sacrifice of Iphigenia—expands its overtones to the total scale of
tragic action, and surrounds the present event—Agamemnon's
death—with the resulting resonances of meaning and emotion. The
Fool also generalizes, but through a process of reduction, and surrounds the present event with laughter. In the instance I have

chosen, he also proceeds to a clear insight rationally expressed. Lear's kingship is reduced to a matter of eggshells; an extreme is posited opposite Lear's sense of his importance; through this juxtaposition of extremes, a middle ground is reached on which Lear's situation may be accurately evaluated. This middle ground is the realm of Apollonian reason and moderation, which is achieved in the play by a striking balance of opposites. In Act II, Lear will find Kent in the stocks and himself refused access to Regan:

LEAR. O me, my heart, my rising heart! But down!
FOOL. Cry to it, nuncle, as the cockney did to the eels when she put 'em i' the paste alive. She knapped 'em o' the coxcombs with a stick and cried "Down, wantons, down!" [II, iv, 132–36]

Here, indeed, is the equilibrium of steel springs pulling with equal force in opposite directions.

The spectator senses this radical version of Apollonian moderation; Lear does not. But the Fool leads him, again and again, to the edge of that abyss which the blinded Gloucester will eventually seek, led by a man who is as mad as the Fool is foolish. It is not called "fate," or "the gods," but Nothingness. When Goneril first enters with a frown, the Fool tells Lear: "Now thou art an 0 without a figure. I am better than thou art now: I am a fool, thou art nothing" (I, iv, 189–91). Goneril's frowning face turns to frowning speech, and Lear asks one of the play's central questions:

LEAR. Does any here know me? This is not Lear.
Does Lear walk thus? speak thus? Where are
his eyes? . . .
Who is it that can tell me who I am?
FOOL. Lear's shadow.
LEAR. I would learn that. [I, iv, 222–29]

Learn it he does, in time, though he will also pass beyond his nothingness to the nothingness of man, and beyond even that.

King Lear: Acts II, III

As Lear confronts the "0 without a figure," his speeches (and the language of the play in general) become increasingly rank with images of nature—frequently a violent or corrupted nature. We are

far from the sacred grove of the Furies in *Oedipus at Colonus*.
Here is Dionysus the hunter, who dismembers calves on Mount
Cithaeron, or the savage, erotic nature of Phaedra's imagination.
It is a nature in which Lear finds metaphors for his rage, and beneath whose blows he will transcend both that rage and himself—
in madness and wisdom. His individuality will be annihilated in
nature and nothingness, in a Dionysiac exultation wedded to pain.

Lear calls on nature to aid his cause against Goneril:

> Hear, Nature, hear! dear goddess, hear!
> Suspend thy purpose, if thou didst intend
> To make this creature fruitful.
> Into her womb convey sterility;
> Dry up in her the organs of increase.   [I, iv, 277–81]

And again, in thick-piled images:

> You nimble lightnings, dart your blinding flames
> Into her scornful eyes! Infect her beauty,
> You fen-sucked fogs, drawn by the powerful sun,
> To fall and blister!   [II, iv, 182–85]

He calls for a vengeance from the skies which is linked to kindness:

> If you do love old men, if your sweet sway
> Allow obedience, if you yourselves are old,
> Make it your cause! Send down, and take my part!
>   [II, iv, 214–16]

Yet nature is more than a guiding order, or an external instrument;
it also dwells within men. The unkind Goneril is

> . . . a disease that's in my flesh,
> Which I must needs call mine. Thou art a boil,
> A plague sore or embossed carbuncle,
> In my corrupted blood.   [II, iv, 249–52]

The unnatural daughters are as natural as disease, and it may be
that nature is their goddess, as it is that of Edmund. Both good
and evil call on nature for their warrant and aid.

Man is part of the natural order, but with a difference. Lear argues
with Goneril and Regan over the number of followers he will be
allowed:

REG.   What need one?

LEAR. O, reason not the need! Our basest beggars
Are in the poorest thing superfluous.
Allow not nature more than nature needs,
Man's life is cheap as beast's.   [II, iv, 297–301]

Natural man is nothing, and the encounter with nature on the
heath will become an encounter with nothingness. Lear has called
upon the heavens; turned out of doors by his daughters, he will
hear an answer. Act II ends with the storm in full force in Act III.

Lear no longer calls upon the elements for aid, but for a general
curse embracing even him:

Blow winds, and crack your cheeks! rage! blow!
You cataracts and hurricanoes, spout
Till you have drenched our steeples, drowned the cocks!
You sulph'rous and thought-executing fires,
Vaunt-couriers of oak-cleaving thunderbolts,
Singe my white head! And thou, all-shaking thunder,
Strike flat the thick rotundity o' the world,
Crack Nature's molds, all germens spill at once,
That make ingrateful man!   [III, ii, 1–9]

Nature is summoned even to its self-destruction in a vision echoed
by our modern discoveries of exploding galaxies or the law of en-
tropy. Lear, however, demands a purpose, however terrible, behind the forces of destruction. Heaven's fires are "thought-executing." Perhaps their thoughts are unkind to man, yet he cannot
accuse them:

I never gave you kingdom, called you children,
You owe me no subscription. Then let fall
Your horrible pleasure. Here I stand your slave,
A poor, infirm, weak and despised old man.
[III, ii, 17–20]

Lear no longer asks if the heavens "do love old men" (II, iv, 214).
They owe nothing to him, yet he does not (as he might) regard
them as purely indifferent aggregations of matter. If nature is not
beneficent, and yet remains purposeful, it must be malevolent:
"I call you servile ministers,/ That will with two pernicious daughters join/Your high-engendered battles" (III, ii, 21–23).

Kent enters amid nature's lightnings and declares, "Man's na-

ture cannot carry/ The affliction nor the fear" (III, ii, 48–49).
Here is an apprehension of that which is unbearable to man, like
the wisdom of Silenus which is transformed into a song of praise
by Dionysiac man. Lear himself will bear the unbearable, or bear
himself beyond it. First, he must see beyond himself—he must see
the Fool. Kent speaks to him of shelter, and Lear turns to the
shivering, unimportant man beside him: "Come on, my boy. How
dost, my boy? Art cold?/ I am cold myself" (III, ii, 71–72).

At the hovel, the Nature outside contracts to the nature within.
The winds still rage for Lear, and there is no hiding place in his
soul:

> Thou thinkest 'tis much that this contentious storm
> Invades us to the skin. So 'tis to thee;
> But where the greater malady is fixed,
> The lesser is scarce felt. . . .
> . . . The tempest in my mind
> Doth from my senses take all feeling else
> Save what beats there.   [III, iv, 10–19]

The thought of his daughters' ingratitude beats there, as it beat
before, and "that way madness lies" (III, iv, 26). Yet it is joined
to another thought, whose path will follow through madness and
beyond it:

> Poor naked wretches, wheresoe'er you are,
> That bide the pelting of this pitiless storm,
> How shall your houseless heads and unfed sides,
> Your looped and windowed raggedness, defend you
> From seasons such as these? O, I have ta'en
> Too little care of this! Take physic, pomp;
> Expose thyself to feel what wretches feel,
> That thou may'st shake the superflux to them
> And show the heavens more just.   [III, iv, 35–43]

Suddenly, Lear's individuality is absorbed in a Dionysiac insight
which transcends his particular situation. The Dionysiac moves
the individual *beyond himself*; it involves the shattering of the
principium individuationis. In the storm, Lear's suffering begins to
embrace the suffering of all "naked wretches," and his pity begins
to transcend self-pity. In the Dionysiac state, "each individual be-

comes not only reconciled to his fellow but actually at one with him." [18] The process is evident in the king's relation with the Fool, and, perhaps more emphatically, in his dialogues with "Tom o'Bedlam." Lear merges with his fellowman at the zero point of being, in his nothingness.

The transformation in Lear is radicalized by the circumstances under which it occurs. The king is attended by the palpable violence of nature and three actors, the unreal and the real: Kent has surrendered his name to follow a king who is no king; the Fool is an actor who bears only the name of his role, and his foolishness is wisdom; Edgar has surrendered both his name and the appearance of sanity, because he has seemed to be what he is not—a traitor to his father. All three appear, from one point of view, as lesser men than they are: the noble and the wise play beggars and fools. Yet there is a level on which they merge with their roles: noblemen and wise men alike are wretches insofar as they are men betrayed by others and assaulted by the heavens. On this level, the play within a play which they create becomes a true image of reality.

Lear provides the most important link between the inner play's illusion and the reality which it reflects. Confronted with Edgar's feigned madness, he becomes mad in earnest; but Lear's madness, like the Fool's foolishness, will be more than it seems—the escape from reality will in fact be a profound *confrontation* with the reality of man's condition.

Although Edgar's madness is feigned, it is closer to the self-absorption which we tend to associate with mental disease. Tom o'Bedlam sees his private fiends and torments, and little else; Lear sees the portraiture of his suffering in Tom, and pities him:

EDG. Who gives anything to poor Tom? whom the foul fiend hath led through fire and through flame, through ford and whirlpool . . . Tom's acold. O, do de, do de, do de. . . .
LEAR. Have his daughters brought him to this pass?
Couldst thou save nothing? Wouldst thou give them all?

[III, iv, 57–69]

Earlier, the Fool told us how "The hedge-sparrow fed the cuckoo so long/That it's had it head bit off by it young" (I, iv, 212–13).

Now Lear speaks of "Those pelican daughters" (III, iv, 81), finding a model in nature for unnatural behavior. In *Batman uppon
Bartholome* (ed. 1582), we discover this account of the legend:

The Pellican loueth too much her children. For when the children
bee haught, and begin to waxe hoare, they smite the father and
the mother in the face, wherefore the mother smiteth them againe
and slaieth them. And the thirde daye the mother smiteth her
selfe in her side that the bloud runneth out, and sheddeth that
hot bloud uppon the bodies of her children. And by virtue of the
bloud the birdies that were before dead, quicken againe.[19]

More is visible here than the violence of children against their
parents. The pelican kills its young, and later gives its own blood
for their resurrection, on "the thirde daye," which is like that third
day when Christ is resurrected. The love and violence of natural
creatures is viewed in the context of the sacred and the transcendent. In this context, it assumes a universal validity, echoes a universal mystery.

Lear is, of course, in error: Edgar has no daughters. But his
father has been betrayed by a son, and, in his error, smites another
son with whom he will later be reconciled at the point of death,
when his heart bursts "smilingly" (V, ii, 237). The Dionysiac affirmation of this death is implicit in nature itself, in the inscrutable order of the world, which embraces both the pelican's love and
its hate, both death and resurrection.

Tom o'Bedlam, Edgar's mask, is also, paradoxically, fundamental
man beneath the mask called "Edgar," or man reduced to his fun-
dament, "that eats the swimming frog, the toad, the todpole, . . .
that in the fury of his heart, when the foul fiend rages, eats cow-
dung for sallets, swallows the old rat and the ditch-dog" (III, iv,
131–34). Lear sees him fully, with compassion, and through him,
sees himself and all men:

Is man no more than this? Consider him well. Thou owest the
worm no silk, the beast no hide, the sheep no wool, the cat no per-
fume. Ha! Here's three on's are sophisticated! Thou art the thing
itself; unaccommodated man is no more but such a poor, bare,
forked animal as thou art. Off, off, you lendings! Come, unbutton
here.   [III, iv, 107–13]

Tom is "the thing itself," the 0 without a figure, the nothingness of man which Lear at last apprehends. Lear has heard, in his torment, the advice of Silenus:

Ephemeral wretch, begotten by accident and toil, why do you force me to tell you what it would be your greatest boon not to hear? What would be best for you is quite beyond your reach: not to have been born, not to *be*, to be *nothing*. But the second best is to die soon.[20]

The play could, indeed, end with this insight. It does not so end, because Shakespeare has not exhausted the subject. Nietzsche, speaking of the Greeks, tells us that the relation of the Olympian gods to the wisdom of Silenus "is that of the entranced vision of the martyr to his torment."[21] A similar vision, a like affirmation, will emerge in *King Lear*. Both the old king and logic were mistaken when they declared that "nothing will come of nothing" (I, i, 95).

Like Job on the ash heap, Lear cannot curse God and die, that is, despair. Unaccommodated man assumes, in his person, the judge's robes. The heavens have been silent amid cries for justice, and so a 0 without a figure will hold a trial. The trial is—nothing; a play within the play within the play, in which the masks of Edgar and Kent and the Fool assume the further masks of justices, illusion piled on illusion. And the defendants?

> FOOL. Come hither, mistress. Is your name Goneril?
> LEAR. She cannot deny it.
> FOOL. Cry you mercy, I took you for a joint-stool.
>
> [III, vi, 50–52]

The court is powerless; only wood can be called to answer for wooden hearts, and it is dumb. Bitter laughter fills the stage.

> LEAR. And here's another, whose warped looks proclaim
> What store her heart is made on. Stop her there!
> Arms, arms! sword! fire! Corruption in the place!
> False justicer, why hast thou let her scape?
>
> [III, vi, 54–57]

The illusion of Regan's presence is followed by the illusion of her flight; even in the realm of imagination, the trial collapses. One more defendant is arraigned, but does not appear; Lear asks, "Is there any cause in nature that makes these hard hearts?" (III, vi, 78–79).

Shakespeare plucks us suddenly from a vision of justice as compounded illusion to a real injustice so extreme that it seems unreal. Gloucester has aided Lear; in the next scene, the eyes are plucked from his head by Cornwall, and he is sent to "smell/His way to Dover" (III, vii, 109–10). Yet here, at the point where Chaos seems enthroned over the world, Cosmos begins to assert itself: France and his powers are approaching, and Cornwall is wounded to the point of death by his own servant. At the end of Act III, this exchange occurs between humble men:

> 2. SERV. I'll never care what wickedness I do,
>   If this man come to good.
> 3. SERV.   If she live long,
>   And in the end meet the old course of death,
>   Women will all turn monsters.
>   [III, vii, 116–20]

Evil has become intolerable, a weed which threatens to infect the gardens of the world if it is not plucked. Like Herod and all the villains of medieval drama, Cornwall, Regan, Goneril, and Edmund are destined to fall. But they carry Lear—and Cordelia—with them, as if sentence could only be executed by burning the courtroom and all its inhabitants. The end of the tale will raise as many questions as it answers.

King Lear: Act IV

Edgar begins the act with his own vision of the comfort inherent in nothingness:

>   To be worst,
> The lowest and most dejected thing of fortune,
> Stands still in esperance, lives not in fear.
> The lamentable change is from the best;
> The worst returns to laughter. Welcome then,
> Thou unsubstantial air that I embrace!   [IV, i, 2–7]

In a movement typical of the play, this insight founded on bitter experience, this painful synthesis, suddenly confronts a new fact which shatters it. Gloucester enters, his eyes still bleeding. The "unsubstantial air" is poisoned, there is something worse than the worst of fortune, and a man of nothing, in the mad arithmetic of the world, can still be split in two:

> But who comes here?
> My father, poorly led? World, world, O world!
> But that thy strange mutations make us hate thee,
> Life would not yield to age.   [IV, i, 10–13]

Unlike Lear, Gloucester does not begin his exile by calling on the heavens for aid. He has his reasons: "As flies to wanton boys are we to the gods./They kill us for their sport" (IV, i, 44–45). Yet even here, in the teeth of his own words, Gloucester searches for order, for intelligibility, for the forms of heavenly justice. He gives a purse to Tom o'Bedlam:

> That I am wretched
> Makes thee happier. Heavens, deal so still!
> Let the superfluous and lust-dieted man,
> That slaves your ordinance, that will not see
> Because he does not feel, feel your power quickly;
> So distribution should undo excess,
> And each man have enough.   [IV, i, 80–86]

The Apollonian illusion of order, of universal coherence, crumbles beneath a single fact: Gloucester is speaking to his unhappy son. It is with the full burden of this irony that we are carried into the next scene, and Albany's comment on Goneril:

> If that the heavens do not their visible spirits
> Send quickly down to tame these vile offenses,
> It will come,
> Humanity must perforce prey on itself,
> Like monsters of the deep.   [IV, ii, 52–56]

Albany, too, affirms a universal order, and seemingly with more cause than Gloucester—he learns of Cornwall's death.

> This shows you are above,
> You justicers, that these our nether crimes
> So speedily can venge!   [IV, ii, 89–91]

Yet the voice turned upwards in faith descends again: "But O poor Gloucester!/Lost he his other eye?" (IV, ii, 91–92). Every cadenced affirmation of universal order is followed by new dissonance, and the Lear music proceeds in all its harsh splendor, still unresolved.

But, again—there is Cordelia. When a Gentleman speaks of her to Kent, the monsters of the deep seem, for a moment, very distant:

> And now and then an ample tear trilled down
> Her delicate cheek. It seemed she was a queen
> Over her passion, who, most rebel-like,
> Sought to be king o'er her. . . .
> . . . Patience and sorrow strove
> Who should express her goodliest. You have seen
> Sunshine and rain at once: her smiles and tears
> Were like. . . .
> Sorrow would be a rarity most beloved,
> If all could so become it.   [IV, iii, 13–26]

The Apollonian harmony of Cordelia mediates the drama's Dionysiac extremities of passion into a realm of unearthly translucence which seems to affirm a sacred order. The Gentleman tells how (like a saint in a world ruled by the medieval God) "she shook/ The holy water from her heavenly eyes" (IV, iii, 33–34). The vision will be resurrected later, in Cordelia's reconciliation with Lear. For the moment, we see the lady herself, confirming the Gentleman's description by her actions (IV, iv). Only a brief glance at Regan's intrigues (IV, v) separates this scene from our next, fantastic encounter with Gloucester and Edgar.

Like Lear's judgment of Regan and Goneril, the scene begins with a play within a play, and Edgar, mad justice of the mock trial, is the stage manager of a mime.

The Elizabethan stage is bare and flat. We see two men on the boards, bent with effort, lifting one leg above the other, climbing, yet never rising:

> GLOU. When shall I come to the top of that same hill?
> EDG. You do climb up it now. Look how we labor.
> GLOU. Methinks the ground is even.

EDG.   Horrible steep.
  Hark, do you hear the sea?   [IV, vi, 1–5]

On the surface, we are asked to accomplish no more here than
what the Chorus demands in *Henry V*: to piece out the "imper-
fections" of a physically limited stage with our thoughts, and think,
when the drama speaks of horses, that we "see them/Printing
their proud hoofs i' the receiving earth" (Prol., 26–27). The cathedral of Elizabethan drama is built of imagination, not bricks and
mortar.

Yet here, uniquely, Shakespeare seems to be drawing our attention to the theatrical illusion *as such*, and in a rather complex way.
We are asked to believe, within the conventions of the play *King
Lear*, that we see Gloucester and Edgar on level ground somewhere near Dover, too far from the cliffs for the sea to be audible.
At the same time, the dialogue, normally a vehicle for the imaginative creation of the "real" scene, establishes an imaginary landscape as vivid as the storm on the heath in Act III. From the cliff's
edge,

> . . . How fearful
> And dizzy 'tis to cast one's eyes so low!
> The crows and choughs that wing the midway air
> Show scarce so gross as beetles. Halfway down
> Hangs one that gathers sampire—dreadful trade!
> Methinks he seems no bigger than his head.
> The fishermen that walk upon the beach
> Appear like mice.   [IV, vi, 15–23]

As spectators, we see two actors on a level stage. Like Edgar, we
know the scene takes place on level ground near Dover. However,
we are also, like Gloucester, blind men before whose inner eyes
the abyss opens in all its terrible splendor. Gloucester renounces the
world, and plunges over the edge. How are we to interpret the
plunge? Jan Kott proposes this answer: "The blind Gloucester who
has climbed a nonexistent height and fallen over on flat boards, is
a clown."[22] He is only partially right. Gloucester has really cast
himself into an abyss—one which exists in inner, not outer space.
Even Edgar is, for a moment, swayed by the illusion of his father's
death: "Thus might he pass indeed" (IV, vi, 57).

Gloucester wakes to new strength, resurrected in spirit: "Henceforth I'll bear/Affliction till it do cry out itself/'Enough, enough,' and die" (IV, vi, 90–92). Although his theological frame of reference is (as the play's setting demands) pagan, he is not unlike the Christian who spiritually dies to the flesh to be reborn in Christ. Kott discusses the relation of this scene to Christian drama:

Gloucester . . . is no longer a court dignitary whose eyes have been gouged out because he showed mercy to the banished king. The action is no longer confined to Elizabethan or Celtic England. Gloucester is Everyman, and the stage becomes the medieval *Theatrum Mundi*. A Biblical parable is now enacted; the one about the rich man who became a beggar, and the blind man who recovered his inner sight when he lost his eyes.[23]

One basic qualification must be added; a qualification which sets us beyond the mysteries. Edgar tells his father that his companion on the cliff above was a demon, and adds: "Think that the clearest gods, who make them honors/Of men's impossibilities, have preserved thee" (IV, vi, 88–89). On a literal level, the gods' miracle is as illusory as the demon. The sacred source of order and miracles, so certain in the medieval world-picture, is shrouded in mystery and doubt in *King Lear*.

Kott describes the outer journey of Gloucester, which is also that of Lear:

Everyman begins his wanderings through the world. In medieval mystery plays also the stage was empty, but in the background there were four mansions, four gates representing Earth, Purgatory, Heaven and Hell. In *King Lear* the stage is empty throughout: there is nothing, except the cruel earth, where man goes on his journey from the cradle to the grave.[24]

On the empty stage, the paths of Gloucester and Lear cross. The Earl has risen, renewed, from his plunge into an imaginary abyss. Lear has gone deeper, much deeper into his: the formless, savage, and yet redemptive Dionysiac abyss of madness. The cruel earth has tutored him, and the transformation begun under the buffetings of the storm has been completed. Tom o'Bedlam and the Fool are no longer necessary; both have disappeared from the action, and yet Lear embodies them. Like Tom, he is mad; like the Fool, he is the Chorus commenting on man's passage and the brazen ironies of the world.

Once again, Lear holds a trial, and the judge is a king,

> Ay, every inch a king!
> When I do stare, see how the subject quakes.

And yet:

> I pardon that man's life. What was thy cause?
> Adultery?
> Thou shalt not die. Die for adultery? No.
> The wren goes to it, and the small gilded fly
> Does lecher in my sight.   [IV, vi, 123–29]

This time, the judge will not pass judgment, he will not act. We find a reason for this inaction in *The Birth of Tragedy*:

While the transport of the Dionysiac state, with its suspension of all the ordinary barriers of existence, lasts, it carries with it a Lethean element in which everything that has been experienced by the individual is drowned. This chasm of oblivion separates the quotidian reality from the Dionysiac. But as soon as that quotidian reality enters consciousness once more it is viewed with loathing, and the consequence is an ascetic, abulic state of mind. In this sense Dionysiac man might be said to resemble Hamlet: both have looked deeply into the true nature of things, they have understood and are now loath to act.[25]

Lear's madness is a departure from self grounded in the self's agony; as such, it combines Dionysiac "oblivion" with a continued perception of quotidian reality. This perception, however, places Lear *beyond* action, beyond the act of judgment. Lear sees a pervasive evil at the heart of being which destroys the meaning of particular judgment:

See how yond justice rails upon yond simple thief. Hark in thine ear. Change places and, handy-dandy, which is the justice, which is the thief?   [IV, vi, 166–69]

Nietzsche ascribes this, the still point of Dionysiac insight, to Hamlet; it is also visible in Macbeth when his wife dies; and here, affirming its general significance for Shakespeare's tragic vision, we find it in Lear's madness.

Yes, Lear has perceived truth and its terror, but another, a re-

demptive vision seems to lie beyond it. The Gentleman who comes
to bring Lear to his daughter speaks these lines:

> . . . Thou hast one daughter
> Who redeems nature from the general curse
> Which twain have brought her to.   [IV, vi, 221–23]

A daughter, and her husband—and their army, which may restore
the unweeded garden of the state.

The scene comes in the midst of busy preparations for the battle,
a stillness in the eye of the storm. Lear has slept at last. He wakes,
under Cordelia's gaze, a king, though he knows better what he is:

> COR. How does my royal lord? How fares your Majesty?
> LEAR. You do me wrong to take me out o' the grave.
>   Thou art a soul in bliss; but I am bound
>   Upon a wheel of fire, that mine own tears
>   Do scald like molten lead.
> COR.   Sir, do you know me?
> LEAR. You are a spirit, I know. Where did you die?
>   [IV, vii, 50–56]

In Lear's vision of the world, won through extremest suffering, a
Cordelia is not part of the natural order, and therefore unable to
survive—in short, dead and transformed into a spirit. Cordelia
thinks his wits are still wandering, but the play's end will validate
Lear's terrible insight. And yet—we have not reached the end:
There will be the moment of beauty first, the lone flower on the
heath before the deadly storm. It transfigures the play, as it must.
The Fool's bitter laughter is gone, and warm tears, like a spring
rain, unburden the turbulent clouds:

> LEAR. . . . Do not laugh at me;
>   For (as I am a man) I think this lady
>   To be my child Cordelia.
> COR.   And so I am, I am.
> LEAR. Be your tears wet? Yes, faith. I pray weep not.
>   If you have poison for me, I will drink it.
>   I know you do not love me, for your sisters
>   Have, as I do remember, done me wrong:
>   You have some cause, they have not.
> COR.   No cause, no cause.
>   [IV, vii, 77–86]

The cadences fall gently, and nature, or at least a meaningful portion of it, is redeemed from the general curse. All that was implied in the faithfulness of Kent and the Fool, in Edgar's patience, finds its summation in Cordelia's two quietly repeated phrases.

The sun has blessed the bleeding earth. Now the storm will break.

King Lear: Act V

The change of mood, of scene, is startling. The transition to the last act makes us profoundly aware of the differences between Shakespeare's theater and the Greek stage. Instead of the linear, inevitable flow of actions and images, there are lamps set at sharp angles, illuminating the contradictions of their inevitable center: the ground of human life and action, and, beyond, the mysterious ground of all Being.

In Act IV, Lear woke to the sight of Cordelia; Act V springs to life with the sound of drums, and Edmund and Regan in the midst of their intrigues. It is virtually impossible, at this point, to view the sisters' competition for Edmund, and his own duplicity towards them, as merely one more *particular* evil; Lear's suffering, and the sheer Gothic *multiplicity* of evils, like a corridor of demons carved in stone, directs our vision to the universal implicit in the particular.

Consider, for a moment, the second scene in Act V, where the playwright who wrote *Henry V* presents a major battle of remarkably short duration. At the beginning of the scene, Edgar brings his father to a tree to wait out the battle, telling him to "pray that the right may thrive" (V, ii, 2). *Six lines later* he enters with this news: "King Lear hath lost, he and his daughter ta'en" (V, ii, 7). The promise of a coherent universe has collapsed as if it never existed. Gloucester speaks:

> GLOU. No further, sir. A man may rot even here.
> EDG. What, in ill thoughts again? Men must endure
>   Their going hence, even as their coming hither;
>   Ripeness is all. Come on.
> GLOU.   And that's true too.
>   [V, ii, 9–13]

Only the bitter willingness to endure is left to man now. Yet, mysteriously, Lear sees something more in defeat. His reconciliation with Cordelia is a fact which cannot be defeated, and Lear plucks a beauty from it, quietly:

> . . . Come, let's away to prison.
> We two alone will sing like birds i' the cage.
> When thou dost ask me blessing, I'll kneel down
> And ask of thee forgiveness. So we'll live,
> And pray, and sing, and tell old tales, and laugh
> At gilded butterflies, and hear poor rogues
> Talk of court news; and we'll talk with them too,
> Who loses and who wins; who's in, who's out;
> And take upon's the mystery of things,
> As if we were God's spies; and we'll wear out,
> In a walled prison, packs and sects of great ones
> That ebb and flow by the moon.   [V, iii, 9–20]

This vision of the mortality of "great ones" arises from just that insight into human nothingness which plunged Lear raging into madness. Yet here it is seen differently, without bitterness, from the mountain peak of the Chinamen in Yeats' "Lapis Lazuli":

> On all the tragic scene they stare.
> One asks for mournful melodies;
> Accomplished fingers begin to play.
> Their eyes mid many wrinkles, their eyes,
> Their ancient, glittering eyes are gay.[26]

Here is the affirmation inherent in Dionysiac wisdom, the entranced vision of the martyr in the midst of his torments. Lear transcends the apprehension of truth and its terror, and he does so through what Nietzsche calls "the spirit of the sublime, which subjugates terror by means of art."[27] The king plots a play within the play, with Cordelia and himself as protagonists. In that play, prison is not what it seems, but a realm in which quotidian existence is suspended, where history is viewed from the superior vantage point of an Eternal Present saturated, like the Kingdom of Heaven, with love. Here Lear and Cordelia will "pray, and sing," outside time, while the mighty of the earth "ebb and flow by the moon."

If God is necessary to the medieval drama of redemption, Cordelia is necessary to Lear's drama of the imagination. "He that parts us," declares the royal playwright, "shall bring a brand from heaven/And fire us hence like foxes" (V, iii, 24–25). His words suggest that a more than human force is needed to divide them, that the heavens themselves must savagely intervene. Then father and daughter depart to their prison.

Once again, the play is saturated in the quotidian world; under the ebb and flow of the moon, Edmund gives advice to a Captain: "Know thou this, that men/Are as the time is" (V, iii, 34–35). There will be a death in captivity. Now the good have fallen, and the evil rise to battle each other; both Regan and Goneril lust for Edmund. Yet there is still hope for the future. Albany has learned of his wife's duplicity, and Edgar, disguised, emerges to fight Edmund. He wins. After the defeat of Cordelia's army, it seems almost a miracle, almost the assertion of a Divine Order.

The fallen Edmund asks the name of the man who has defeated him, and hears this answer:

> My name is Edgar and thy father's son.
> The gods are just, and of our pleasant vices
> Make instruments to plague us.
> The dark and vicious place where thee he got
> Cost him his eyes.   [V, iii, 205–9]

Edmund answers: "Th' hast spoken right; 'tis true." There is, it would seem, a justice governing the world. Gloucester's blindness was punishment for a sin, like Edmund's defeat. Yet we remember that the immediate reason for Gloucester's blindness was his kindness to Lear. Edgar's justification of the gods is incomplete.

But the action proceeds, for a while, as if governed by Providence. Edmund has fallen; now we learn that Regan has poisoned Goneril and stabbed herself. The chain of evil seems broken by what Albany calls "this judgment of the heavens" (IV, iii, 276). The order of love implied in Lear's reconciliation with Cordelia has been repeated in Edgar's reunion (his identity revealed) with Gloucester:

> I asked his blessing, and from first to last

> Told him my pilgrimage. But his flawed heart
> (Alack, too weak the conflict to support!)
> 'Twixt two extremes of passion, joy and grief,
> Burst smilingly.   [V, iii, 233–37]

Again, we are in the radiant eye of the sun. Even the bastard feels
its rays. When the bodies of Regan and Goneril are brought in,
he speaks like one transfigured by grace:

> Yet Edmund was beloved. . . .
> I pant for life. Some good I mean to do,
> Despite of mine own nature. Quickly send
> (Be brief in't) to the castle; for my writ
> Is on the life of Lear and on Cordelia.
> Nay, send in time.   [V, iii, 287–95]

In a play where evil seemed absolute, we hear the voice of repen-
tance proceeding from love. Edmund's defeat seemed to prove the
justice of the heavens; now we hear the tone of their gentler
grace. Only for a moment.

The judgment of audiences during the hundred and sixty years
when Nahum Tate's version of *King Lear* held the stage was, in a
sense, correct.[28] The play's ending is intolerable, unbearable. It
may prove illuminating to glance, briefly, at Tate's happy ending,
in which Cordelia is saved and Lear lives, and Gloucester's heart
does not burst. Lear's final speech runs thus:

> No, *Gloster* Thou hast business yet for Life;
> Thou, Kent, and I, retir'd to some close Cell,
> Will gently pass our short reserves of Time
> In calm Reflections on our Fortunes past
> Cheer'd with Relation of the prosperous reign
> Of this celestial Pair; Thus our Remains
> Shall in an even Course of Thought be past
> Enjoy the present Hour, nor fear the Last.[29]

Here is a reflection (however distorted) of the Lear whose transfigured vision saw a jail as paradise, the Lear who has gained wisdom
through suffering. Edgar (who is to rule with Cordelia) ends the
play with this praise for Lear's one perfect daughter:

> Thy bright Example shall convince the World

(Whatever storms of Fortune are decreed)
That Truth and Vertue shall at last succeed.[30]

A superficially Christian moral concludes the tale. The world is intelligible, and good, in spite of everything, wins out in the end. The "clearest gods" (IV, vi, 88) of which Edgar speaks do exist, and there is no contradiction at the heart of Being. Man's suffering is the purgatorial fire of a Divine Comedy which ends in redemption. In this sense at least, Tate is closer to the medieval world-picture than Shakespeare, though he is more distant from it in time and in the breadth of his vision.

Shakespeare could, perhaps, have chosen to end his play happily, and done so in great poetry. He has, after all, repeatedly plunged us into the abyss of terror, of chaos, of suffering, and raised us up again to a vision of order, of redemption. It is superfluous to say that the play would then not be a tragedy; we should have to dismiss the *Oresteia* on the same grounds. The fact is that Shakespeare ends *King Lear* with the death of Cordelia and Lear. They do not die of the fifth act, but necessarily; and we must explore that necessity.

Under the gracious heavens, Edmund repents, and evil is merciful. Amid this brightness, the storm breaks. An old, weak, defeated king enters like a giant in agony, carrying a daughter in his arms:

Howl, howl, howl! O, you are men of stones.
Had I your tongues and eyes, I'd use them so
That heaven's vault should crack.   [V, iii, 307–9]

Here is the Lear of Act III, naked under the savage heavens, lamenting; Lear before the metamorphoses of his madness, Lear before his reconciliation with Cordelia. The king's wisdom won through extremest suffering, his calm above the storms of the world, has been shattered upon the irremediable event. Cordelia is dead.

Edgar could see Gloucester's lechery as the cause of his fall, and we may trace Lear's destruction to his foolishness and pride, though the punishment, in both cases, is very much out of proportion to the crime, as if the ruling gods were patterned on Angelo in *Measure for Measure*. But the death of Cordelia is grotesque, unfair. The only "crime" of which she might be accused is lack of hypocrisy in the first scene of the play. Her death is outrageous, and we can only conclude that Shakespeare wants us to be outraged. Against whom? Regan and Goneril are dead, and the repentant Edmund is dying. In the last scene of his tragedy, Shakespeare has eliminated all the evil *individuals* against whom our anger might be directed. Again, we must conclude that the playwright did this with some purpose in mind, and not through oversight; we can grant no less to the craftsmanship of one of our greatest dramatists.

The outraged eye of the spectator turns from the scene of desolation, barren of villains, to "heaven's vault" arching over it, and from specific evil to what Kitto calls "Evil itself."[31] The death of Cordelia compels us to embrace, in its terrible finality, a general vision toward which the entire play has been moving. Edmund, the instrument of this death, is irrelevant; when his end is announced, Albany dismisses the event: "That's but a trifle here" (V, iii, 356). And Lear greets the news of his other daughters' death with only an "Ay, so I think" (V, iii, 351). The mystery of evil gapes huge above its fallen, mortal instruments.

Kent perceives this when he asks, "Is this the promised end?" (V, iii, 314). There is a savage irony implicit in the question. The "promised end" is the Second Coming of medieval Christianity, the point at which history ceases and God's eternal present becomes visible, the moment of judgment when the evil fall to Hell and the blessed are raised to eternal salvation. It is the last scene of the medieval mysteries, warrant and seal to all the scenes that have preceded it, and cause for joy in the good man. Here, instead, is universal lamentation, and Cordelia fallen with her evil sisters.

Albany attempts to establish the old Cosmos in the midst of Chaos, declaring: "All friends shall taste/ The wages of their virtue, and all foes/ The cup of their deservings" (V, iii, 364–66); but he is only, after all, a feeble, mortal judge, not the Judge Himself; and Lear's voice rises above his, crying to Cordelia:

> And my poor fool is hanged! No, no, no life!

> Why should a dog, a horse, a rat, have life,
> And thou no breath at all? Thou'lt come no more,
> Never, never, never, never, never!   [V, iii, 367–70]

Like Agave bent above the body of her dismembered son, he sees
that the pieces will not join again. No one attempts to reassure
him that Cordelia now dwells with the souls in bliss; if he once
saw man as "a poor, bare, forked animal" (III, iv, 112), he now
sees a Cordelia who is less than a living dog or rat. He has reached
down, more fully than ever before, to the dregs of the terrible
wisdom of Silenus, a martyr robbed even of the hope of Heaven.

Here, in the tragedy's final abyss of being, Lear searches, beyond
hope, for a sign of breath on Cordelia's lips, searches absurdly:

> Pray you undo this button. Thank you, sir.
> Do you see this? Look on her! look! her lips!
> Look there, look there!   *He dies.*
> [V, iii, 371–73]

It is perhaps the most remarkable moment in the history of drama.
We remember Gloucester, whose heart, when he recognized his
son, "'Twixt two extremes of passion, joy and grief,/ Burst smilingly" (V, iii, 236–37). That was only a figure of Lear's death,
its shadow. The old king has encountered ultimate nothingness,
the final zero of Being, and from it plucked something, everything, a breath on Cordelia's dead lips, the entranced vision of
the martyr in his torment. His illusion, like the hand of a god, has
created the world from original Chaos.

Lear's life ends with an affirmation, but a paradoxical one. His
redemption, like that of Oedipus in the grove of the Furies, is individual, personal. The end of Oedipus, however, left a blessing on
the state, a promise of safety for Athens, if not Thebes or his
daughters. Lear leaves only the bleeding earth, the silent heavens,
the stricken features of men, and an incomprehensible affirmation.
Wearily, Albany calls on Kent and Edgar for the restoration of
order:

> ALB. Rule in this realm, and the gored state sustain.
> KENT. I have a journey, sir, shortly to go.
> My master calls me; I must not say no.

EDG. The weight of this sad time we must obey,
Speak what we feel, not what we ought to say.
[V, iii, 386–90]

No Fortinbras comes on stage in triumph, to bind the wounds of society. The scene is as desolate as the end of the *Bacchae*, except for Lear's transfigured vision.

Tragic Ontology in the *Lear* Universe

The problem of being in *King Lear* is tied to the medieval problem of the existence of evil along with good in a universe ruled by an omnipotent God. Saint Augustine solves the latter problem by associating good with being, evil with nonbeing: "All things which suffer corruption are deprived of something good in them. Supposing them to be deprived of all good, they will cease to exist altogether." Human wickedness "is not a substance but a perversity of the will turning away from you, God, the supreme substance, toward lower things." [32] It is, in other words, a movement by man toward lower orders of the great chain of being.

In the medieval mysteries, such a distinction is difficult to maintain, since stage demons, for example, are seen with the same substantial form as men or angels, and Hell-mouth asserts a *theatrical* claim to being at least as great as that of the structures representing Heaven.[33] Here we are apt to see two kingdoms, ruled over by God and Satan, respectively, contending for man, though we are confident that the Kingdom of God will triumph in the last act.

In *King Lear*, the process is carried a step farther. The contending forces still exist, but they are no longer visible kingdoms. Demons and angels are spoken of, but not seen. Only man, good, wicked, or both—only man is visible, and the earth on which he acts and suffers. On this stage, Cordelia and her sisters define the polarities of good and evil. Significantly, they issue from the same parents. In the same way, all good and evil in the play proceed under the one arch of nature, to which all characters, Edmund as well as Lear, appeal for their justification or for justice. Good and evil alike seem to emanate from nature and the gods: the storm which assists Regan and Goneril in their purpose leads Lear to self-knowledge; the chance which defeats them destroys Cordelia. Behind this we see not the Supreme Being, Good itself, but the tragic, contradictory ground of Being. In this vision, *King Lear* displays its affinity with Greek tragedy, while proceeding from an examination of the medieval problem of good and evil.

Roughly speaking, the *Lear* universe bears the same relation to the medieval world-picture as the Euripidean universe bears to the world-picture implied at the end of the *Oresteia*. For Aeschylus, the relation of man to the universe and the gods was mediated by the polis, which resolved the contradictory demands of Apollo and the Furies. Euripides witnessed the disintegration of the polis, and saw man, without its mediation, torn by the Dionysiac contradictions of an irrational universe and its irrational gods. For the Middle Ages, the principle of unity was not the state, the city of man, but God's radiant oneness, resolving all human and natural contradictions, including particular good and evil, in an unchanging and perfect eternity. In *King Lear*, God has become invisible or nonexistent, and only an image of the mediator Christ is visible in Cordelia, who does not rise from the cross of her death; and man is torn by the unmediated wars of good and evil.

What is the ontological status of the tragic hero in the *Lear* universe? To answer this question, we must turn again to the Middle Ages. I have already quoted Eliade's observation that through faith, "Christianity translates the periodic regeneration of the world into a regeneration of the human individual." [34] This regeneration takes place when man acknowledges God and his own nothingness before God. St. Paul declares that "God hath chosen the foolish things of the world to confound the wise; and God hath chosen the weak things of the world to confound the things which are mighty" (I Cor. 1:27). We have seen Lear sound the depths of his nothingness, and, "weak" and "foolish," grow to inner power and a meaningful wisdom. The Christian "history" of individual salvation forms the center of a play set in pagan times and written in an age which reflected a disintegration of the theological certainties of the Middle Ages, an age of exploration, scientific discovery, secular learning.

But how do we account for Lear's final moment over the body of Cordelia, his vision of life-in-death at the instant of his death? To place this in a Christian context, we must look forward in time to Kierkegaard, or far back, beyond the systematic theology of Aquinas, to Tertullian's *De Carne Christi:*

The Son of God was crucified; I am unashamed of it because men must needs be ashamed of it. And the Son of God died; it is by all means to be believed, because it is absurd. And He was buried and rose again; the fact is certain because it is impossible.[35]

Lear ends his life with an absurd act of faith; and its absurdity is greater than that of Tertullian's faith in Christ, since it is contradicted by visible fact as well as reason. Nevertheless, it is a faith which redeems the world.

The absurd act is not isolated, an appendage to the play: it is implicit in all that has gone before. The whole history of Lear's "Christian" regeneration has proceeded in a universe barren of Christ, witnessed only by man and brute nature. The Christian derives his being through the spiritual imitation of Christ's archetypal crucifixion and resurrection: "We are buried with him by baptism into death: that like as Christ was raised up from the dead by the glory of the Father, even so we also should walk in newness of life" (Rom. 6:4). The archetype which Lear imitates, however, is neither Christ nor a pagan god or hero acting *in illo tempore,* but "unaccommodated man" (III, iv, 111)—essential man, stripped of the accidents of time and place and custom, nakedly confronting the universe which has engendered him. That universe is visibly a chaos—savage, formless, a terrible witches' brew of lust and cruelty. In his discussion of archaic man's periodic regeneration of temporality, Eliade notes that the celebration of a New Year involves the ritual "repetition of the mythical moment of the passage from chaos to cosmos," the imitation of the original moment of the world's creation.[36] Lear's descent into nothingness is a descent into original chaos, from which Lear constructs a vision of order and redemption, a subjective version of cosmos.

In the *Oresteia*, the subjective and objective versions of chaos and cosmos are wedded. Thus Orestes, at the end of *The Libation Bearers*, suffers mental torments which reflect a chaos in the world-order—the conflicting claims of Apollo and the Dionysiac Furies. In the *Eumenides*, the cure of his personal malady is associated with the resolution of these conflicting claims. The movement from chaos to cosmos, to unity of being, is both a subjective and an objective fact. As in the *Oresteia*, there is an act of judgment knit into the fabric of the last scene of *King Lear*. Cordelia and all that she embodies—the cosmos of order, of goodness, of love—must live or die. If she lives, says Lear, "It is a chance which does redeem all sorrows" (V, iii, 318). Lear makes his absurd choice, and establishes, on a subjective level, the movement from chaos to cosmos, to unity of Being. But Cordelia is objectively dead, and the chaotic universe does not confirm the transition; we are still "upon the rack of this tough world" (V, iii, 378). Lear's solution is even more personal than that of Sophocles' Oedipus, since the sacred grove of his imagination has no substantial reality, and he leaves no blessing on the state. Like the medieval Christian, he can, in the final analysis, redeem only himself, and each man bears his own burden of salvation. If the Christian is granted God's grace, Lear is granted, from some invisible source, his transfiguring illusion.

Lear's plunge into essential truth and its terror—the abyss of Dionysiac perception in which his *principium individuationis* is annihilated in the archetype of essential, "unaccommodated man" —leads to his uniquely *individual* Apollonian illusion of order; and the illusion can be named: Cordelia lives. Here is the play's tragic wedding of the Apollonian and the Dionysiac, a wedding which assumes subjective form. Beneath Lear's archaic pattern of redemption, objective history and its quotidian terrors continue; there is no evidence that they will be objectively redeemed by the Second Coming of a Christ, when, as in the last play of a medieval cycle, the good are raised and the wicked cast down. I have, in the course of this chapter, noted a number of similarities between *King Lear* and medieval drama, but this is the point at which

Shakespeare departs most profoundly from that divinely comic world.

If *King Lear* is modeled after a medieval cathedral, its roof is in ruins and open to every storm, and the statues of the saints are broken. At the end of the aisle down which Lear stumbles bareheaded is a chalice cracked but still golden in the darkness, lit by a single ray of light from a shattered window.

Suffering and Time: The Breath on Cordelia's Lips

One passage in *The Birth of Tragedy* describes the lyric poet, who is,

first and foremost, a Dionysiac artist, become wholly identified with the original Oneness, its pain and contradiction, and producing a replica of that Oneness . . . [which] becomes visible to him again, as in a dream similitude, through the Apollonian dream influence. . . . The artist had abrogated his subjectivity earlier, during the Dionysiac phase: the image which now reveals to him his oneness with the heart of the world is a dream scene showing forth vividly, together with original pain, the original delight of illusion. The "I" thus sounds out of the depth of being; what recent writers on esthetics speak of as "subjectivity" is a mere figment.[37]

There are important similarities between Nietzsche's lyric poet and King Lear; and Lear is, in this sense, an artist within a work of art—the play which bears his name. Like the lyric poet, Lear abrogates his initial subjectivity (whose limitations led him into error) to absorb himself in the Dionysiac insight of the storm scene. At the end of the play, the pain of this insight is transfigured by illusion; Lear sees a replica of the Oneness of being "as in a dream similitude," and in that dream, Cordelia breathes. Although the illusion takes a *particular* form, it is not, in Nietzsche's sense, "subjective," since it carries the full resonance of Dionysiac insight.

Yet there is an important sense in which Lear's illusion *is* subjective. Oedipus' final illusion of redemption in the grove of the Furies is validated by the *Colonus* universe, which reports it as fact; the "illusion" envelops the total aesthetic artifact, the play itself. In contrast, the last scene of *King Lear* presents us with a play within a play, and the illusion of the "lyric poet" Lear within the dramatic illusion, which affirms that Cordelia is dead while Lear affirms the opposite. Here Lear's insight must be regarded as a very special kind of subjectivity, personal and limited when set against the dramatic illusion of Cordelia's death, and at the same time universal and formative, creating an order from the visible chaos of the *Lear* universe.

The play presents a particular history of suffering, a particular sequence of painful events in the quotidian world. Its characters continually search for a transhistorical meaning for this suffering, in the eternal order of the gods or nature—Lear's final moment is only the most extreme, paradoxical version of this search. His illusion, like that of Nietzsche's lyric poet, transcends time and suffering. If we, as spectators, accept that vision, the world is ecstatically redeemed in our eyes. If we see only Cordelia's corpse, Lear's affirmation is absurd, grotesque, the error of a deluded man who dies a meaningless death in a world whose history follows no coherent pattern, reflects no transhistorical meaning.

There is a third possibility. The spectator may accept Lear's illusion *and* acknowledge Cordelia's death, participate in Lear's ecstasy and recognize the temporal fact which negates it. In the first perspective, he will see Lear's affirmation sounding from the depth of being, a confirmation of the world's eternally repeated passage from chaos to cosmos, the archaic repetition of the world's creation *in illo tempore*. The second perspective is historical and secular; here time and the event are irreversible and Lear's subjectivity is limited: a particular man's particular illusion at a particular time and place.

The distinction is not oversubtle. Earlier, I considered two concepts central to the medieval, Christian world-picture: first, the picture (derived from the Hebrews) of linear, irreversible history, which signified a change from the normally anhistorical world-picture of the Greeks; second, the redemption of man's historical suffering, and the "valorization" of his existence, in a transhistorical realm—God's eternal present. The paradox inherent in the two poles of this world-picture is explored in *King Lear*. The exploration is not abstract, but it is, in a meaningful way, philosophic. Lear affirms the archaic ontology which the Middle Ages held in common with Hellenic Greece; much of the play in which he acts and suffers affirms the historicism which the Middle Ages holds in common with the modern world. In this sense, the choice between Cordelia dead and Cordelia living is the choice between two conceptions of man's being. If Shakespeare does not make the choice, it may be because, giantlike, he embraces both.

· THE TRAGEDY OF HISTORICAL MAN ·
FROM HEGEL TO IBSEN

> The only Thought which Philosophy brings with it to the contemplation of History, is the simple conception of *Reason;* that Reason is the Sovereign of the World; that the history of the world, therefore, presents us with a rational process.
>
> HEGEL, The Philosophy of History

IT IS difficult to determine with any accuracy the century in which Western civilization became fully *historical,* abandoning archaic ontology and its sacred rituals of repetition. Historicist tendencies are, as I have shown, visible in Hellenic Greece, though they are not of major importance. The medieval *figura* accepts the concrete uniqueness of the historical event, while discovering its significance in God's anhistorical kingdom; and the Wakefield mystery cycle follows historical sequence while mentioning Christ before his temporal birth. Historicism is thus present in the Middle Ages, but it is by no means of predominant importance. The Renaissance embraces both of the medieval tendencies, and they influence Shakespeare's tragic (and comic) art to an extent which I have only crudely indicated in an examination of one play. In general, the Middle Ages and the Renaissance do not present a fully developed conception of modern, historical man, who is also, in an important sense, secular man, stripped of a transhistoric sacred reference for his actions.

Eliade states what is, for him, the important period of transition: "From the seventeenth century on, linearism and the progressive conception of history assert themselves more and more, inaugurating faith in an infinite progress, a faith already proclaimed by Leibniz, predominant in the century of 'enlightenment,' and popularized in the nineteenth century by the triumph of the ideas of the evolutionists."[1] However, Carl L. Becker's *Heavenly City of the Eighteenth-Century Philosophers* is devoted to the proposition that the "enlightenment" was in fact engaged in constructing a new version of the medieval world-picture.[2] And in *The Discovery of Time*, Stephen Toulmin and June Goodfield, writing from the perspective of modern science, suggest that historical man did not fully emerge until well into the nineteenth century, though his way was prepared earlier:

In the years immediately before 1800, Johann Gottfried Herder was writing about historical development in the same manner as his contemporary, Lamarck. . . . The course of cosmic history was, for both men, a single directed process which, as time went on, created more highly-developed organisms and societies in progressive sequence. . . . Herder thus took the first step toward a more historical conception of the world, but the second step was more difficult—that of recognizing that the actual course of history was too complex to be fitted into any simple teleological scheme. Herder's ideas established a tradition of philosophical history which was developed during the next half-century by Hegel, Comte and Marx. . . . What Herder saw as the realization of the purposes of Mother Nature, Hegel interpreted as the self-development of *Geist* or Spirit.

The authors add that, however,

after the establishment of modern historical criticism and Darwinian theory, it would be naive to suppose any longer that history represents either a *single* process, or one with a demonstrable *direction*. . . . If there is a key to the understanding of all history, it consists in recognizing not its single-directedness, but rather its multiple opportunism. In this respect, even Marxism looked backwards to Lamarck rather than forwards to Darwin.[3]

Although historicism developed before Darwin, it maintained a teleological structure which could still grant a value to historical man and his suffering, while disposing of him and his works in the inevitable forward movement of time. Hegel's discussion of "World-Historical persons" embodies this double perspective, which suggests that some elements of the medieval world-picture have been preserved, in altered form, in the new historicism.[4]

In spite of his teleological assumptions, it is impossible to deny the importance of Hegel as a seminal formulator of the qualities and significance of historical man. In addition, he has had an important influence on modern drama. Eric Bentley has observed that the dramatic criticism of Friedrich Hebbel, heavily influenced by Hegel, is "more closely linked with the history of high drama in Europe than that of any of his contemporaries"; and Robert Brustein cites his influence on Ibsen, the central figure in modern prose tragedy.[5]

For the moment, I wish to consider two assertions made by Hegel in *The Philosophy of History*: First, "The only Thought which Philosophy brings with it to the contemplation of History, is the simple conception of *Reason*; that Reason is the Sovereign of the World; that the history of the world, therefore, presents us with a rational process." Second, "Nothing has been accomplished without interest on the part of the actors; and—if interest be called passion, inasmuch as the whole individuality . . . is devoted to an object with every fibre of volition, . . . we may affirm absolutely that *nothing great in the World* has been accomplished without *passion*." Reason dominates history, whose events contribute to the concrete evolution of its dialectic. At the same time, events proceed from human action, which proceeds from individual passion, which is a means to the ends of history:

Two elements, therefore, enter into the object of our investigation; the first the Idea, the second the complex of human passions; the one the warp, the other the woof of the vast arras-web of Universal History. The concrete mean and union of the two is Liberty, under the conditions of morality in a State.[6]

What does Hegel mean by Liberty and the State? To understand this, we must first look at his definition of Spirit. It is the opposite of matter, which is composite; "it seeks its unity" and "strives after the realization of its Idea," so that it is "the essential destiny of Reason." Briefly, "Spirit . . . may be defined as that which has its centre in itself." Furthermore, "Universal History . . . is the exhibition of Spirit in the process of working out the knowledge of that which it is potentially," Spirit evolving to complete self-consciousness and self-contemplation.[7]

In these terms, Freedom belongs truly to Spirit rather than the individual:

Spirit is *self-contained existence* (Bei-sich-selbst-seyn). Now this is Freedom, exactly. For if I am dependent, my being is referred to something else which I am not; I cannot exist independently of something external. I am free, on the contrary, when my existence depends upon myself.[8]

Hegel's version of historical man, freed from the repetition of archetypes, is nevertheless bound by "something external"; only Spirit is truly free. In another passage, Hegel relates these notions to the idea of the State:

In the history of the World, only those peoples can come under our notice which form a State. For it must be understood that this latter is the realization of Freedom, i.e. of the absolute final aim, and that it exists for its own sake. It must further be understood that all the worth which the human being possesses—all spiritual reality, he possesses only through the State. . . . For Truth is the unity of the universal and subjective Will; and the Universal is to be found in the State, in its laws, its universal and rational arrangements.[9]

At the same time, the State is different from particular states (and civilizations), which are abandoned and replaced in the historical process through which Freedom realizes itself in the world. Hegel speaks of the larger sphere of History, in which

are presented those momentous collisions between existing, acknowledged duties, laws, and rights, and those contingencies which are adverse to this fixed system; which assail and even destroy its foundations and existence; whose tenor may nevertheless seem good —on the large scale advantageous—yes, even indispensable and necessary. These contingencies realize themselves in History: they involve a general principle of a different order from that on which depends the *permanence* of a people or a state. This principle is an essential phase in the development of the *creating* Idea, of Truth striving and urging towards consciousness of itself. Historical men—*World-Historical Individuals*—are those in whose aims such a general principle lies.[10]

Here, indeed, lie the seeds of the social dramas of Hebbel, Ibsen, Brecht, and countless other modern playwrights. Men can change the state, alter the fabric of society. However, they are also, like the status quo which they alter, dispensable, and must give place to the next step in the historical process.

What relation does Hegel's historicism bear to the tragic antinomies, the Apollonian and the Dionysiac? Recall, for a moment, the philosopher's distinction between universal Reason and individual passion. Then consider this passage from *The Birth of Tragedy*:

He lays his dramatic plan as Socratic thinker and carries it out as passionate actor. So it happens that the . . . drama is at the same time cool and fiery. . . . It cannot possibly achieve the Apollonian effects of the epic, while on the other hand it has severed all connection with the Dionysiac mode; so that in order to have any impact at all it must seek out novel stimulants. . . . These stimulants are, on the one hand, . . . ideas put in the place of Apollonian contemplation, and on the other fiery emotions put in the place of Dionysiac transports.[11]

Nietzsche is speaking here of Euripides, who, as I suggested earlier, is an eminently *Dionysiac* dramatist whose purpose and methods were as misunderstood by Nietzsche as they were by Aristotle. However, his words remain largely valid as a portrait of post-Hegelian historicist tragedies—Hebbel's *Maria Magdalena*, for example, or Ibsen's *Ghosts*. Here is the distinction between a Hegelian (or "Socratic") rationality, the master plan of action, and the individual "passionate actor" in history or the drama.

There is an important difference between reason and the Apollonian, and between passion and the Dionysiac, though the terms are related. Hegel sees reason as a universal process fulfilling the purpose of Spirit—that completed state of self-consciousness which is characteristic of a "self-contained existence," the truly ontic, the ground of Being. On another level—which is that of Hegel the philosopher, or Socrates, or (to a considerable extent) the modern scientist—reason is man's way of discovering and exhibiting the laws of a rational universe. Implicit here is Hegel's larger assumption that the universe *does* display a rational structure. The modern astronomer might well find Hegel's metaphysic superfluous; he would on the other hand, claim that the earth will circle the sun again next year, and if it does not, there are definite, intelligible *reasons* for the failure; if the reasons are not known, it is only because man has not yet advanced far enough in his knowledge of the laws of stellar physics.

Apollonian "reason," on the other hand (and this is a distinction of profound importance), does not assume that the order of the universe is rational. Faced with the disorder of experience, it *creates* simplicity, clarity, the illusion of a finite perfection—the sculpture of Praxiteles instead of Hegel's tortuously rational *Philosophy of History* or the equations of mathematical physics. The Apollonian is also, therefore, the domain of individuation, whereas reason is independent of the individual.

A related contrast is visible between passion and the Dionysiac. Hegel sees passion as ontically limited, individual, a means by which particular persons are driven to fulfill the purposes of reason in the world. The modern logical positivist A. J. Ayer, proceeding from scientific principles of objective verification, goes even beyond Hegel in declaring that the passions are literally meaningless, and therefore unworthy (except in a very limited sense) of philosophic study.[12] Here passion is relegated to the realm of limited subjectivity. This is a common attitude in the scientific framework of modern, historical man. In contrast, Dionysiac passion is closer to the broader meaning of Greek physis—the "unwritten, unconditionally valid 'natural law,' against the particularism of local custom."[13] Dionysiac man, far from being lost in his personal, limited passion, absorbs himself in the elemental, contradictory "passion" of the ground of Being itself, original Oneness, the truly ontic. He expresses, that is, the suprarational truth of a suprarational universe.

Behind these contrasts lies a difference between two major attitudes toward experience. Nietzsche assigns them to "the artist" and "theoretical man":

While the artist, having unveiled the truth garment by garment, remains with his gaze fixed on what is still hidden, theoretical man takes delight in the cast garments and finds his highest satisfaction in the unveiling process itself, which proves to him his own power. Science could not have developed as it has done if its sole concern had been that one naked goddess. For then the adepts of science would have felt like people trying to dig a hole through the earth, each of whom soon realizes that though he toil in lifelong labor he will excavate only an infinitesimal fraction of the great distance and that even this fraction will be covered over before his eyes by another's efforts.[14]

In this respect, Hellenic Greece belonged to the party of the artist, with its gaze, amid the exploration of truth, fixed on the mystery at the heart of Being; and medieval Christianity, aware, like Dante's Vergil, of the point beyond which reason cannot pass, acknowledged the ultimate mystery of God. Theoretical man is modern man, the scientist or historian whose work becomes a footnote to those who follow him. Here Newtonian mechanics falls before relativistic mechanics, which, in turn, discovers its limitations in quantum mechanics. Hegel, that optimistic theoretical man, thought he had dug to the center of intelligible truth, but his efforts represent an abandoned excavation for much of modern philosophic history.

What is the nature of tragic drama in the world of theoretical man, historical man? The question has no single, simple answer. There are, on the one hand, plays whose point of view is essentially historical. I cannot help but feel that these works are limited as tragedies. A great deal of discussion has been devoted to the question of whether, for example, the protagonist of *Death of a Salesman* can be regarded as a tragic hero, since he is an ordinary man rather than a king. Such a formulation of the question seems to me very much beside the point; this, however, is important: we understand the suffering of Willy Loman as something that could be remedied by social change. In contrast, the suffering of Lear or Oedipus is, in a very basic sense, beyond remedy, since it involves basic contradictions at the heart of the eternally real, the ground of Being.

If the tragic vision of historicism is necessarily limited, modern man is not necessarily limited to a historicist viewpoint. Nietzsche, for example, observes how

science, spurred on by its energetic notions, approaches irresistibly those outer limits where the optimism implicit in its logic must collapse. For the periphery of science has an infinite number of points. Every noble and gifted man has . . . come up against some point of the periphery that defied his understanding. . . . When the inquirer, having pushed to the circumference, realizes how logic in that place curls about itself and bites its own tail, he is struck with a new kind of perception: a tragic perception, which requires, to make it tolerable, the remedy of art.[15]

Here is a position based on but transcending the sciences of historical man: a perception of the Dionysiac contradictions at the heart of the real arrived at through experience of the contradictions inherent in logic itself. It is reflected in the best plays of Ibsen and Strindberg and, in our own century, in the works of Yeats, Beckett, and Genet.

The preceding pages must serve as a crude overview of the major problems to be encountered in this chapter and the next. It is time to turn to seventeenth-century France, and neoclassical tragedy. The play under consideration is Jean Racine's masterpiece, Phèdre. The play proceeds from the same myth as Euripides' Hippolytus, and a comparison of the two plays will serve to delineate, more sharply than might otherwise be possible, the features of an early version of the tragic art of historical man.

Reason and Passion: Racine's Phèdre

George Steiner describes Phèdre as "the keystone in French tragic drama. The best that precedes it seems in the manner of preparation; nothing which comes after surpasses it."[16] This is, perhaps, excessive praise; Corneille's art is complete in itself, and not simply a preparation for Racine and Phèdre. Nevertheless, the play does stand out as a crucial piece of tragic writing, in which both the virtues and the limitations of an age and its aesthetics are visible in the highest degree.

Stendhal once argued that Shakespeare is a romantic, Racine a classical artist. The distinction has been frequently made by other writers, most of them romantics who, like Victor Hugo, were engaged in writing and defending plays which exhibited many of the mechanisms of Shakespearean drama, but a profoundly more limited vision of reality.[17] To accept such a distinction, I should have to declare that classical Greek drama is *not* classical, certainly not in the sense understood by the artists and critics of seventeenth-century France. Racine's conception of tragic form and meaning has its basic roots in Aristotle and Horace, not the Greek tragedians. The difference is basic. The *Poetics*, for example, tells us more about Aristotle's logic than the "logic" of Greek tragedy: a marriage of the Apollonian and the Dionysiac is viewed within the discursive horizon of the syllogism. From this follows what Francis Fergusson calls "Racine's art of plotting as rational demonstration."[18]

A glance at the preface to *Phèdre* brings the point home, and tells us something of its consequences:

In no other of my plays have I given virtue as exalted a place as in this: the slightest evil is severely punished; the very thought of crime is made as horrible as the commission of it; the weaknesses of love itself are treated as veritable shortcomings; the passions are exhibited with the purpose of showing the disorder into which they lead us; vice is introduced in such wise as to make us detest it in all its horrible deformity. . . . We should like our works to be as . . . full of useful instruction as were those of antiquity.[19]

In these terms, tragic drama becomes something very much like a series of footnotes to the *Nichomachean Ethics* viewed in terms of the Ten Commandments. Of course, Racine's remarks are in part an attempt to soothe the rancor of the moral critics of tragedy, the inevitable puritans for whom the theater has always been the Devil's immoderate breeding ground. Nevertheless, this apology remains an uncommonly accurate description of the rational and didactic content of his art. He accomplished with glorious success what Nahum Tate's version of *King Lear* attempted: the imposition of a rational order on inchoate experience.

Consider the play itself. Euripides' *Hippolytus* brings us immediately to a recognition of the larger scene of the gods enfolding the action: Aphrodite delivers a prologue explaining her anger against Hippolytus and outlining her revenge; then Hippolytus enters, singing his worship to Artemis. The framework is established for a duel between two contradictory elements of the ground of Being, whose Apollonian projections are Artemis and Aphrodite. Racine begins with a dialogue between Hippolytus and his tutor, Theramenes, regarding the whereabouts of Theseus. We first see Hippolytus as a devoted son, not an embodiment of chastity. In fact, we do not learn of his reputation for chastity until, a few lines later, he confesses his new-found love for Aricia, sole survivor of the blood royal of Athens. Euripides' Aphrodite would have no quarrel with this youth, who has already yielded to her. Even Hippolytus' chastity has been reasonable—a reaction against his father's former immoderate lust, with "troth plighted here and there and everywhere."[20] Aristotle, in the *Nicomachean Ethics*, argues that to reach the golden mean in passion from one extreme "we must drag ourselves away to the contrary extreme; for we shall get into the intermediate state by drawing well away from error, as people do in straightening sticks that are bent."[21] This is, precisely, what Hippolytus has done: in reacting against his father's extreme in love, he has found the mean.

His passion, in fact, is immoderate in only one sense; it runs contrary to Theseus' order regarding Aricia: "Her brothers' blood must never flow again/ In a child of hers."[22] Yet that order never attains a compelling importance in the play, and there is no Chorus to suggest the horrors that may befall the state if Aricia marries. The conflict between love and rational duty is here, but it is not posited in its extreme form until Phaedra comes on stage.

In Euripides' play, the Nurse speaks first, and the burden of her words is the mystery in the ground of Being, that "something other dearer still than life/ the darkness hides and mist encom-

passes." But Racine's Phaedra speaks before Oeone: "I am dazzled
with the light; it has been long/ Since I have seen it." [23] The light
of which she speaks is that of reason as well as the sun—the reason
which permeates the ordered world of French tragedy, replacing
Euripides' Dionysiac darkness. Opposed to it is passion:

> In all my fevered body I could feel
> Venus, whose fury had pursued so many
> Of my sad race. I sought to shun her torments
> With fervent vows. I built a shrine for her,
> And there, 'mid many victims did I seek
> The reason I had lost. [24]

It would seem that here, as in Euripides, Aphrodite is active in a
tormented soul. Yet it is a different Aphrodite, invoked but not
visible, and, as we have already seen, variable in her effects: love is
an extreme in Phaedra, but a moderation of chastity in Hippolytus.
Aphrodite is the conventional name for a *subjective* disposition
which manifests itself differently in different individuals, and not
Euripides' absolute principle. For Phaedra, it is a negative rather
than a positive reality, a special deficiency of reason. Opposed to it
is Phaedra's rational duty toward her husband and her children.

It is in this context that we should approach Racine's use of a
false report of Theseus' death, and the queen's reaction to it.
Oeone advises her: "The king is dead, you bear the bonds no
longer/ Which made your love a thing of crime and horror." [25] The
conflict between Phaedra's passion and her rational duty has been
(at least on one level) destroyed. In fact, Hippolytus must be won
over and convinced that, contrary to appearances, he is not hated
by Phaedra, since the death of Theseus may cause him to lead
rebels against his seeming foe, threatening the royal claim of
Phaedra and her son. Reason seems, for the moment, to support
the claims of passion.

When Phaedra declares her love, she is rejected by a Hippolytus
who, unlike his Euripidean counterpart, is an eminent representative of sophrosyne, and willing to own "that I mistook your words,
quite innocent." His reticence stands in vivid contrast to Phaedra's
condemnation of her own passion, her "polluted blood." Reason

and passion have not, after all, been reconciled. Phaedra tells us why when she learns that Athens has voted for her rule: "I reign— And shall I hold the rod of empire,/When reason can no longer reign in me?" [26] Extremes of passion cannot (and here Racine differs from Hegel) contribute to such rational ends as the guidance of a state; rather, there must be harmony between the macrocosm of reason-in-society and the microcosm of reason-in-men. Here *Phèdre* displays its close connection with the principles of the French enlightenment.[27]

The return of Theseus radicalizes the division between extreme passion and rational duty. Phaedra denounces Hippolytus, who will not reveal the truth to his father. In Euripides, Hippolytus does not speak because he has sworn an oath of silence, and does not expect that he would be believed in any case. In Racine, duty toward his father commands silence: "I might be pardoned, should I speak the truth./But it concerns your honor to conceal it." Condemning him, Phaedra has acted as *if* Hippolytus himself stood at a passionate extreme, ready to reveal an offense to his chastity; her passion has blinded her to his moderate reasonableness.[28]

In extreme anger, Theseus banishes his son and pronounces the fatal curse on his life. Euripides ends the scene with a choric song which, characteristically, directs our attention beyond the visible action of the drama:

> I have a secret hope
> of someone, a God, who is wise and plans;
> but my hopes grow dim when I see
> the deeds of men and their destinies.
>
> . . . .
>
> I am angry against the Gods.
> Sister Graces, why did you let him go
> guiltless, out of his native land,
> out of his father's house? [29]

We are continually forced to consider the contradictions inherent in the universal scheme of things, that order which envelops and penetrates the particular pattern of action and suffering before our eyes. Racine, on the other hand, plunges us immediately back into the particular. Phaedra enters, having heard the angry voice of her husband, perhaps ready "to speak in accusation of myself."[30] Theseus reveals that Hippolytus has claimed he loves Aricia, and Phaedra, suddenly jealous, decides not to speak. Yes, there is a difference in *plotting* here between Racine and Euripides, but it has a significance beyond the details of style: the two poets have different views of man and the world-order. Euripides uses a chorus and Racine does not; but Shakespeare, who has no chorus in *King Lear*, uses his characters—the Fool, Edgar, Lear—as vehicles of Dionysiac insight at comparable points in the drama. Racine chooses, instead, to direct our attention to individual psychology— the specific, *subjective* duel between passion and reason in Phaedra's breast. In so doing, he reveals once again that he is not a Dionysiac artist.

Racine presents a final scene between Hippolytus and Aricia, in which the honor and moderate love of both is displayed. They will leave together, and Aricia, who has no reason to love her persecutor, Theseus, will nevertheless not dishonor him by betraying Phaedra's falsehoods. The choice is fatal, but it will not be questioned—a demonstration of the unquestioned sway of rational duty as the drama's principle of order.

After reporting the fall of Hippolytus, "dragged by those horses his hands had fed,"[31] Racine, unlike Euripides, does not bring him on stage to die. In placing the dying, torn and bleeding man before us, reconciled to his father, Euripides makes us doubly aware of the indifference, and, in an important sense, the brutality of the gods. The Artemis who reveals her follower's innocence to Theseus is capable of anger against Aphrodite, but aloof from human suffering; and her vengeance against a sister-goddess will consist of the destruction of another man—the next unlucky enough to be beloved of Aphrodite. Euripides directs us beyond human conflicts to their celestial source. But Racine is interested in the conflict between reason and individual passion, and so he places two passionate individuals before us: Theseus and Phaedra. We see them at the moment of reason's inevitable triumph.

Phaedra's reason has finally overcome her passion, and she confesses the innocence of Hippolytus:

> . . . The sword had long since cut
> My thread of life, but still I heard the cry
> Of slandered innocence, and I determined
> To die a slower way, and first confess
> My penitence to you.

The sword of Hippolytus is not merely an instrument by whose means Phaedra might have committed suicide without confessing; it is a symbol of her passion, its rejection, and the lie for which it stood as evidence; all these have cut her "thread of life"—which is, in a very basic sense, her reason, the principle of subjective as well as objective unity and order. When Theseus declares, "I wish I might be banished from the world,/For all the world must rise in judgement on me,"[32] he is speaking of the rational world of Racine's tragic drama.

In a discussion of *Bérénice*, Fergusson observes that the essence Racine "wishes to demonstrate is the tragic life of the soul as reasoning. Reason is the sole value: reason is always to be obeyed. From this both the selection, and the arrangements of the facts of the story, follow deductively. Such facts will be chosen as will best illustrate the eternal nature of the reasoning soul: i.e., its life as a conflict with passion."[33] The observation is applicable to *Phèdre* as well as *Bérénice*, and, in fact, serves to characterize the French classical theater in its essential posture.

This theater is not a glance backward to the Theatre of Dionysus, but forward to that of modern, historical man. Apollo and Dionysus, still alive in Shakespeare's plays, have yielded their place to reason and passion. If *Hippolytus* ends with a Dionysiac affirmation of the contradictions in the ground of Being, *Phèdre* ends by declaring that Being is lucid and intelligible, always, in the end, affirming its absolute claims over the limitations of subjective, irrational passions. The "valorization" of tragic man's being emerges from his union with the truly ontic, the eternal order of reason, over the resistance of a soul torn by divisive passion. This process can occur without the death of the individual, and so we have Theseus as well as Phaedra, Bérénice as well as Phèdre.

Racine's reason/passion anticipates Hegel's Reason/passion and his contrast between objectivity and subjectivity. It differs, however, in this important sense: passion is set against reason, not posited as the subjective means for the attainment of Reason's objective ends. Furthermore, reason is not the unfolding logic of a universal Spirit's coming to consciousness of itself, but rather something already given in its final form. In this sense, Racine's sense of intelligible Being is closer to Plato than Hegel, static rather than dynamic. French classicism has provided us with the first important tragic image of historical, theoretical man, but it has not completed the leap into the modern world.

Hebbel and Bourgeois Tragedy

Nearly two centuries separate Friedrich Hebbel's *Maria Magdalena* (1844) from Racine's *Phèdre* (1677).[34] Some elements of Hegel's historicism were anticipated by Racine, but Hebbel had the philosopher at hand, and constructed his theory of tragedy on a Hegelian framework. In his hands, the drama of historical man reaches the stage of self-consciousness.

Racine could think that he was imitating the ancients, whereas in fact he was reflecting the values of his age; but Hebbel tells us outright that the drama "is historical, and that art is the highest form of historical recording."[35] He is speaking of the drama of any age—that of Aeschylus or Shakespeare as well as his own—and there is a sense in which we must regard what he says as a truism; dramatists in all times have effectively recorded the values and contradictions inherent in their times. Nevertheless, there are important differences between *Hamlet's* mirror held up to nature and the "Preface to *Maria Magdalena*." The dramatist of historicism characteristically sees his age through a lens, not a mirror—his work is shaped by a particular idea of history. Hebbel's lens was shaped by Hegelian dialectic, Zola's lens by Darwinism, Brecht's by Marxism. But Hegel, Darwin, and Marx were, in their separate ways, philosophers of history, not merely philosophers in history like Aristotle or Aquinas.

There is a difference between looking at one's historical period and looking at it historically—that is, as a transition from what has passed to what will come to be. The Greeks, Shakespeare, and even Corneille and Racine (in whom we find an image of historical man but not of history itself) follow the first procedure; Hebbel and most later dramatists follow the second. The result is a new complex of images of man and his relation to the Universe— images that have resulted in an array of novel dramatic styles, such as Realism, Naturalism, Epic Theater. The realism of Hebbel and of Ibsen in his middle period is historical realism; and Zola's naturalism has its roots in nature as Darwin understood it, not as it was understood by Hesiod or Dante.

Of course, Hebbel's work has its non-Hegelian source. The early eighteenth century saw the birth of what was called *tragédie bourgeoise*. Bentley defines it as "a genre midway between the older tragedy and comedy" which discovered "the tragedy of modern life." [36] Hebbel tells us that his *Maria Magdalena* is a bourgeois tragedy—with a difference. He deplores two practices of the earlier practitioners of the genre, and promises that he will avoid them. First is the use of "all kinds of externalities: lack of money, for example, surplus of hunger; but above all . . . the conflict between the third estate and the first and second estates in love-affairs." Second is the practice of assigning excessively elevated or debased language to the common people. Hebbel's attack on earlier *tragédie bourgeoise* reflects his conscious relation to the tragic tradition. Accidents and externalities give rise to "much that is pathetic, but not tragic, for the tragic must appear from the start as something necessary, as something postulated in life itself, such as death, as something which is utterly unavoidable." It does not matter on what level of society this necessity is displayed, since art is symbolic; it is "a matter of indifference whether the hands of a clock are made of gold or of brass." To put it differently, "in the bourgeois tragedy everything depends on whether the circle of the tragic form is completed, that is, whether the point has been

reached where we no longer care about the fate of a single individual, arbitrarily chosen by the playwright, but are able to see
in that individual fate a fate which is universally human." [87]

Hebbel's circle of the tragic form is completed in all the plays I
have considered in this study; then what distinguishes his bourgeois tragedy from the tragic art of the past? Another question:
If it is a matter of indifference whether the hands of necessity's
clock are made of gold or brass, why does Hebbel choose to work
with the baser metal? The dramatist provides no direct answer,
but speaks instead of his age, the "fluctuations and ruptures in our
public as well as in our private lives," and "the world-wide historical process which is taking place in our day." Bourgeois tragedy is
related to this historical process. It therefore participates, within
the context of a particular age, in the general purpose of drama,
which is "to clarify the existing state of the world and man in its
relationship to the Idea, that is, to that moral center which conditions all things." [38] Hebbel tends to assign a greater significance
to drama than that granted by Hegel, who (not surprisingly)
places philosophy above art; nevertheless, his vocabulary and
habits of thought are typically Hegelian. Hebbel's Idea is essentially that of the philosopher, with this modification: for the concrete needs of the dramatist, the Idea is represented by social institutions, Hegel's Universal which is manifested in the State.

Hegel described the Idea and individual passion as the warp and
woof of Universal History, with passion serving the rational ends
of Spirit. But Hebbel directs our attention to the conflict between
the social Idea and the individual; as T. M. Campbell observes,
"Hebbel's own experience showed him that the social order presented a solid front to all individual encroachments, that settled
tradition is hostile to anything new. This conflict is a necessary
one, since the existence of the social order depends on conserva-
tism, while the individual, with equal right, asserts its particular
direction." [39] The result is, in Hebbel's words, "the unmitigated
suppression of the individual." [40] In these terms, the Universal becomes a rational ethical equivalent to the Dionysiac and its shattering of the *principium individuationis*. Hebbel's tragic antinomies

are the Idea (as manifested in society) and the individual, rather than the Dionysiac and the Apollonian; and tragedy exhibits the shattering of the individual in his (inevitable) opposition to the Idea.

Clearly, Hebbel offers a more fully *historical* view of man than that visible in Racine. The earlier dramatist's conflict between reason and subjective passion has become a duel between the historical Idea and the individual. If seventeenth-century French tragedy exhibits "the external nature of the reasoning soul: i.e., its life as a conflict with passion," Hebbel's bourgeois tragedy attempts to show "the nature of all human action, which as soon as it tries to manifest a personal (*inneres*) motive, always simultaneously releases a resisting motive which is intended to restore equilibrium." [41]

What is the position of *reconciliation* in this vision? "There is no reconciliation," Hebbel writes. "The heroes fall because they are overweening." [42] In the tragic universe of bourgeois realism, there is no breath on Cordelia's dead lips, and the final transfiguring illusion of Lear is merely a delusion.

The "valorization" of the individual's suffering in such a universe is, at best, problematic. Hebbel tells us how "the individual attains form and firmness of character and resolution in the struggle between his personal will and the general will of the world," [43] but this is, at best, cold comfort: the individual's immolation is inevitable, and the Idea is indifferent. Yet here there is an element of ambiguity in Hebbel's thought. The Idea always triumphs, but its social manifestations are subject to historical change, and this change is visible in the parts as well as the whole of society: "a breaking up of general world-wide conditions can appear only insofar as individual conditions are broken up, just as the earthquake cannot appear except through the collapse of churches and houses and the unrestrained inrushing of the sea." [44] In this sense, the rebellion of the individual may appear as a *sign* of social change. Hegel, whose habits of thought are perhaps more optimistic, grants that certain world-historical individuals may actually help to effect a change to the next age, whose coming in some sense validates their inevitable suffering.[45] The modern drama of social change draws, at various times, on both formulations, though the tendency (in Ibsen and Brecht, for example) is toward Hebbel's harsher vision.

Maria Magdalena is a crucial test of his theory of tragedy, and, more generally, of the strengths and limitations of the realistic drama of historical man. As an early instance of the genre, it is perhaps much given to long speeches too eloquent for the characters who utter them, and asides which bow to older theatrical conventions. Nevertheless, Ibsen's *Ghosts* is in some sense implicit in its pages, and Tolstoy's *Power of Darkness*, and even the naturalism of Becque's *Les Corbeaux*.

Consider the cast of Hebbel's tragedy. There is, first of all, Master Anton, a cabinet maker, a member of the lower middle class; his Wife; his daughter, Klara, who gives the play its name; his son, Karl. In a dramatic tradition stretching back to the *Oresteia*, a family stands at the center of the action. At the periphery are the characters who bring the action to its crisis: a Secretary, Klara's childhood love; Leonard, who has made her pregnant and intends to marry her; Adam, a court bailiff once insulted by Anton; and Wolfram, a merchant. We have come a long way from the kings and queens of the tragic tradition; and the language of the tragic actors is nearly as bare of magnificence as the simple room in which most of the action transpires. Hebbel's timepiece of necessity has hands of brass.

The situation which frames the opening of the play is, again, prosaic. Anton's wife has just recovered from a nearly fatal illness. Klara is secretly carrying Leonard's child. Karl, loved by his mother and despised by his father, has been spending money irresponsibly.

In the first act, Klara's mother falls dead—and Leonard breaks off his engagement—when Karl is arrested for stealing jewels from the writing desk of the merchant. Anton declares that only Klara is left to redeem the house from shame—and to fulfill the rigid morality of the Idea. At the beginning of Act Two, he tells her: "Since your brother is the worst of sons you must become the best of daughters."[46] If she fails, he will cut his throat. When she is at last alone, Klara asks Death to take her, but the merchant interrupts her litany; he has come to declare that Karl is innocent; his wife, who is insane, had hidden the jewels. He also discloses that he had asked for a quiet investigation by Adam, the bailiff, who instead executed his duty with a vengeance. Klara reveals the reason for Adam's hatred. Once, at the tavern, he offered to drink a toast with her father, who "took his glass away and said that people in red coats with blue lapels used to have to drink out of wooden steins . . . and if they wanted to drink a toast with anyone they'd wait till one of their own kind came by." She adds, "And my mother had to pay for this with her death!"[47] Klara does not, however, pursue the consequences of this insight. She merely knows that she is the only one now capable of harming her father.

A reunion with her childhood sweetheart follows—another splintered ray of hope. The Secretary still loves her; Klara reveals her love for him. He sees the God of the Thou Shalt behind society's God of the Thou Shalt Not: "Why should people be left behind? Why should they want to cheat God of the sole tribute that His world yields Him, a happy face and clear sparkling eyes that mirror all the glory of His creation and give it back to Him transfigured?"[48] The vision is a brief one, and falls before the stone fact of Klara's pregnancy. Now even the Secretary agrees that she must marry Leonard. In the last act, Klara goes to Leonard and begs him to marry her, but the Mayor's niece is pregnant by him, and he refuses. Klara leaves, intent on suicide; the Secretary enters, challenges Leonard to a duel. Meanwhile, Karl has returned home. He tells his sister that he will become a sailor, escaping the cramped ethical existence of his father. Klara's mind is elsewhere: "The last thing's done, father's evening drink is on the fire."[49] She leaves to fetch her brother a glass of water from the well. She will not return alive.

That, in brief, is the plot. Its relation to Hebbel's tragic theory is, at least in part, quite clear. Master Anton is the representative of the Idea—the whole complex of traditional social and ethical values. Early in the play, he declares: "The chirping of sparrows can never take the place of the organ for me; when I'm to feel my heart lifted up then I must first hear the heavy iron doors of the church close behind me and imagine them the gates to the world." Here, expressed in a single image, is both the grandeur and the oppressiveness of traditional morality. It includes Anton's generosity to his former Master; but it also asserts that "a man must respect what he has gained through hard labor in the sweat of his brow." Added to this is the pride which Anton displays in his insult to Adam, and the absolute need to maintain the form as well as the substance of ethical perfection: "I can bear up under anything, anything, and I have proved it . . . except shame. Hang around my neck what you like, but don't you touch the nerve that gives me life!" [50]

Although the Idea includes God, it is not a sum of Christian principles, and may embrace, in its social manifestation, a very unchristian idea of pride. Maria Magdalena was forgiven by Christ, but Master Anton would not forgive Klara, just as he does not forgive Karl. There are contradictions inherent in the Idea.

What tragic individual stands opposed to this "original nexus"? The answer is by no means clear. Klara herself has sinned *within* the Idea, and immolates herself according to its demands. Unlike Mrs. Alving in Ibsen's *Ghosts*, she is not crushed by the Idea while attempting to transcend it. She has one moment of profound insight into her condition: "Suddenly I feel like a thousand years old, and time standing still above me, I can't back up and I can't go forward." [51] Leonard's self-seeking amorality is a rebellion against the Idea, and he ends dead by the Secretary's hand; yet his fate is not of central importance. Karl's rebellion, like that of Nora in *A Doll's House*, will carry him beyond the narrow circuit of family and town, but our interest in his fate is overwhelmed by the death of his sister. The Secretary unfolds a new and glorious world to Klara's sight, but then bows to traditional notions of honor and morality.

It seems, in fact, that the characters (except for Leonard) fall because they *fail* to rebel against the Idea; in this respect, *Maria Magdalena* is far more revolutionary than the conservative stance

of Hebbel's tragic theory might lead us to expect. The revolution
is implicit in the last scene of the play. It has been reported that
someone has fallen into the well. Bleeding from a wound sustained
in the duel, the Secretary speaks:

SEC. Now I know why I was struck. It *is* Klara.
ANTON. Go and see! (*seats himself*) I can't. (*Karl goes off*) But
. . . (*rises again*) if I (*to the Secretary*) understood you right
. . . then it has all turned out for the best.
KARL. (*returns*) Klara's dead. She cracked her head horribly on
the rim of the well when she . . . Father, she didn't fall in,
she jumped, a girl saw her!
ANTON. She should consider more carefully before she talks! It's
too dark out there for her to be so certain!
SEC. Do you *doubt* what happened? Yes, you'd like to, but you
can't. Think of what you said to her. You were the one who
pointed out to her the way to her death, and I, I'm the one to
blame for her not turning back. When you suspected her all
you thought about was the tongues that would hiss, but not
about the worthless snakes they belonged to.[52]

Master Anton adheres so absolutely to the Idea that, horribly, he
sees the death of a dishonored Klara as all "for the best," and must
have others regard it as an accident. But now the Idea seems puny;
purged of Hegelian metaphysics, it is reduced to the principle behind the hissing tongues of gossips. The Secretary sees his failure
to rebel fully against that Idea; his anger carries the seeds of a
revolution in morality which would be explored more fully by
Ibsen and Shaw. But Hebbel does not bring us to this point; having
shown the contradictions in the Idea, he leaves us with Master
Anton's final words: "I don't understand the world any more!"[53]

Maria Magdalena established a pattern which would become a
common one in realistic tragedy. It reduces the cognitive sweep
of a Hegelian historicism to the stuffy bourgeois parlor, the wars
of thesis-antithesis to its common inhabitants. There is no room
for reconciliation in such tragedy; the Hegelian synthesis is, at
best, an abstraction which has shed the tragic hero as an abandoned
step of the dialectic of history. We are left with Klara's ugly death,

or Mrs. Alving's speechless horror before her mad son. In the words of Etienne Gilson: "If the realization of the Idea is the march of God through the world, the path of the Hegelian God is strewn with ruins." [54]

Apollo, Dionysus, and their tragic marriage are alien principles in such a world. Instead of the mysterious ground of Being, we are confronted with the intelligible Idea. Subjectivity replaces the balanced clarity of Apollonian individuation. Lear's final vision, which combines both realms, is replaced by a schism between the individual and the Idea, and the tragic hero is stranded on the narrow desert of a particular historical society. With the coming of a Darwinian naturalism, he is individual only in his suffering, since his actions are a product of heredity and environment.

Elizabethan tragedy, building on a medieval world-picture, could include princes and grave diggers, and language both elevated and low, in the compass of its *theatrum mundi*. It could also, as in *King Lear*, include contemporary types—such as Tom o'Bedlam— in a play about a remote historical period. All this was possible because the transcendence of history in an eternal moment of action and suffering annihilates the distinction between one age and another, *sub specie aeternitatis*. In historical tragedy, that which is constant in humanity is still visible, but subordinated to the "accidents" of an historical moment. It is, therefore, hardly surprising that its characters speak prose (and I do not mean the highly charged prose of *Lear*): it is only *sub specie aeternitatis* that men are poets. It is also less than surprising that *Maria Magdalena* and *Ghosts* seem more dated to us than *Oedipus* or *Hamlet*—they embody historical "accidents" different from our own. It is only when historical realism transcends itself that it produces tragedies in the older sense—when it reaches that point at which, in Nietzsche's words, "logic . . . curls about itself and bites its own tail." [55] Ibsen, the master of realistic tragedy, reaches that point in his later plays. *The Master Builder* is perhaps his most complete formulation of a tragic vision founded in realism, but transcending it.

The Transcendental Exposition: Ibsen's
Master Builder

Yes, it is possible to approach *The Master Builder* as an essay in abnormal psychology. Hermann J. Weigand argues that it is necessary "to see Halvard Solness and Hilda Wangel in a naturalistic setting," and so reduces the action "to the psychological interplay of two highly abnormal characters." [56] This analysis occurs in *The Modern Ibsen*; originally published in 1925, the book offers an approach to Ibsen's masterpiece which seems far more dated than the play. Like Ernest Jones' *Hamlet and Oedipus*, it is limited by both the vocabulary and the version of reality offered by a particular contemporary orthodoxy—psychoanalysis. Freudian criticism, like Marxist criticism, may occasionally offer valuable insights into a particular work of dramatic art. On the whole, however, its tendency is to reduce the turbulence of dramatic experience to an arbitrary rational order—and so we have the triumph of theoretical man over art, and of reason over intellect. The supreme irony is that "reasons" change: history, which brought them into being, at last abandons them for new "reasons," and so a Hegelian interpretation of (for example) *Antigone* yields to Freudian and Marxist interpretations, which in turn will yield to something else.

Since much of Ibsen's output (from *Pillars of Society* to *Hedda Gabler*) consists of dramas of social criticism and bourgeois tragedies, the historical aesthetics of Hebbel or Hegel would seem to provide a firmer foundation than does psychoanalysis for a study of *The Master Builder*. Halvard Solness may be seen as the individual standing in opposition to the Idea—the God whose churches he will not build—and destined to be crushed for his opposition. The difficulty here is that Solness also assumes the repressive function of the Idea in relation to younger men—like Ragnar—who also wish to assert their individuality. Furthermore, there is a very real sense in which Solness ends in triumph rather than defeat; and his victory is not that of Hegel's world-historical man: he does not usher in a new order of society, a new period of history. His paradoxical triumph, like that of Lear, is a distinctly personal accomplishment, and at the same time a revelation of the ineffable heart of the real—the ground of Being.

One of the most striking characteristics of the play is its use of the art of exposition. The conventional purpose of exposition is, according to one dictionary of literature, "to convey, while holding audience interest, essential information as to events before the play, as to what the situation is at curtain-rise."[57] This is its function in *Maria Magdalena*, and in the theater of modern realism generally. Exposition fills in "the facts," gives motives for the present actions of the characters—preferably as unobtrusively as possible, but, if necessary, via the proverbial maid dusting in the parlor at the opening curtain. In some cases—in Ibsen's *A Doll's House* or *Ghosts*, for example—the exposition may emerge with considerable subtlety as the play proceeds, significantly woven into the texture of action and dialogue.

The device is also used in Greek tragedy: *Oedipus the King* is, in a sense, entirely exposition, a gradual revelation of what happened to Oedipus before the play began. Yet it is also much more. The exposition of events reveals their divine background, the contradiction in the ground of Being which fashions Oedipus' doom. The exposition of realistic tragedy illuminates the visible action, but in Greek tragedy the exposition also reveals the Dionysiac darkness surrounding that action.

I wish to suggest that *The Master Builder* uses exposition in just this way, transcending what Fergusson saw in *Ghosts*—"the limitations of the bourgeois parlor as the scene of human life."[58] Ibsen's use of exposition emerges clearly from a close examination of the play's action.

Act One. Our curiosity "as to what the situation is at curtain-rise" is immediately aroused by old Brovik's words: "I must have it out with . . . the *Boss*." The source of his anger is not revealed; he and his son, Ragnar, retreat to the draughtsmen's office when they hear footsteps; his niece, Kaja, remains behind. Master Builder Solness enters the workroom; he is, according to the stage directions, "a middle-aged man but strong and vigorous."[59] He whispers to Kaja and strokes her hair. Again, a puzzle—the girl clearly does not share her uncle's rage against the man. A discussion between Solness and Brovik follows, providing a piece of exposition for which Ibsen has skillfully prepared us. Brovik, who is ailing, wishes before he dies to see his son build on his own, but Solness has never offered the youth a word of encouragement. We learn that Solness once worked for Brovik as Ragnar is now working for Solness: "You pushed your way up—outstripping me and all the others!" Now Ragnar too has an opportunity to make his reputation: a married couple is willing to give him the commission to build their house; they consider Ragnar's plans "new and original." But first Solness must approve the drawings. He refuses: "Halvard Solness is to think about retiring now! He must make room for younger men—for the youngest of all, perhaps. He must make room—room—room!" [60] The first stage of exposition is nearly completed. We know that Solness has been holding down his assistant, perhaps fearful that he will be outstripped as he outstripped old Brovik. But what part does Kaja play in all this? We learn in the next scene that Ragnar loves her and hopes to marry her; and Solness, who tells Kaja that she must not leave him, nearly lets slip his reason for it, which will be revealed before long in a scene with the family physician—Solness is using Kaja as a magnet to keep Ragnar working for him.

The situation is clear, "the facts" are on the table. We have been exposed to an excellent example of realistic exposition.

Next, a discussion with Dr. Herdal. Here the exposition begins to darken. Herdal's suggestion that the nervous, delicate Mrs. Solness is disturbed by Kaja's presence leads Solness to explain how he is using her, and how she came to work for him:

SOLNESS: . . . One day Kaja Fosli came here to the office. . . . When I saw how infatuated Ragnar was with her, it occurred to me that if I were to give her a job here, I might get him to stay on too . . . I never said a word about it at the time. I just looked at her, and wished with all my might that I could persuade her to work here. . . . and then she went away. . . . Well, the next day, toward evening—after old Brovik and Ragnar had gone home—she came here again, and behaved as if we'd come to some agreement.

HERDAL: Agreement? What about?

SOLNESS: About the very thing I'd had in mind the day before—though I had actually never said a word about it.

HERDAL: That was strange—[61]

Indeed, it *is* strange. For the first time, we are presented with a piece of exposition which suggests that forces are at work in the universe which cannot be explained realistically. Gradually, from this point, the dialogue and action will take on a density which sinks them beneath the quotidian world of historical man, into the seas of Dionysiac perception. It does not happen at once; the conversation with the Doctor, the rational man, continues. Solness reveals that he has allowed his wife to regard him as a philanderer as an act of penance, but does not reveal why his penance is necessary. He suggests that she thinks he is mad, and adds: "Who knows? Perhaps, in a way, she may be right."[62] The label *seems* a clue to the Master Builder's obsession; will it be supported by the play?

At first, the answer seems affirmative. Solness speaks of his phenomenal luck as a Master Builder, and his fear that the luck will turn:

SOLNESS: . . . I feel the day approaching. . . . You'll see, Doctor—one of these days the younger generation will come knocking at my door—

HERDAL (*Laughing*): Well, what if they do?

SOLNESS: What if they do? That will be the end of Master Builder Solness.[63]

At that precise moment, there is a knock at the door, and a girl dressed in hiking clothes enters—Hilde Wangel, who will in fact urge Solness to the act which results in his death. Hilde is no young architect, and both Solness and the Doctor are amused by the timing of her entrance, which seems a coincidence to them. But it is no coincidence to Ibsen—it is a *fact* of the play's universe, a fact which evades merely rational explanation, like the circumstances surrounding Kaja's employment. In this context, the Master Builder's "madness" consists of his connection with an invisible realm beneath the surface of quotidian reality. It is only in terms of this realm that Hilde's appearance—and her purpose—become intelligible. Like Gerd, the wild mountain girl in Ibsen's early poetic drama, *Brand*, Hilde is a messenger of truths that are not for village wits or the "reason" of historical man.

Scribean drama and the realism which borrowed its techniques thrived upon coincidence, the possible but improbable event which often greased the wheels of the "well-made play." In *The Master Builder* it transcends this function, mediating between levels of reality. If the timing of Hilde's entrance is a coincidence, so was her meeting at a sanatorium with the wife of her childhood idol, and Mrs. Solness' invitation "to come and see her if ever I came to town." [64] The coincidence establishes a realistic basis for her visit, but calls that basis into question when added to other, improbably *frequent* coincidences. Ibsen uses a convention of dramatic realism to cast doubt on its historical-rationalistic view of events. Exposition, normally a device for giving us the "true history" preceding the stage action, undergoes the same transformation. In Ibsen's play, this rational, "secular" history is combined with a suprarational, "sacred" history which transcends it, transforming event into myth.

When Solness—ten years before the action—built a church tower at Lysanger, he climbed the scaffolding to its top to crown it with the traditional wreath. He grew dizzy because a schoolgirl in the crowd below cried up at him, waving her flag wildly. The girl was Hilde:

HILDE: It was so wonderfully thrilling! It didn't seem possible to me that any Master Builder in the whole world could build such a tremendously high tower. . . . And to know that you weren't in the least bit dizzy . . .
SOLNESS: How could you be so sure that I was not—?
HILDE: You dizzy? Of course not! I knew that with my whole being! Besides—if you had been—you could never have stood up there and sung.
SOLNESS (*Looks at her in amazement*): Sung? Did I sing?
HILDE: Of course you did!
SOLNESS (*Shakes his head*): I've never sung a note in my life.
HILDE: Well—you sang then! It sounded like harps in the air. [65]

The mythic and the realistic version of the event are set side by side; Hilde advances the first of these, to which Solness opposes the second. According to one version, a man subject to vertigo once set a wreath upon a tower he had built; according to the other, an ideal Master Builder crowned an ideal tower, singing his triumph with a voice more godlike than human. The conventions of realism demand that we accept Solness' version of the event, but the rational order which it implies has already been called into question by the play, and so our judgment is momentarily suspended.

Hilde proceeds, with conviction and vivacity, to tell the Master Builder that he later came to her house to visit, found her alone in the room, called her a princess, promised that he would return in ten years to carry her off to a distant kingdom, and then kissed her—many times. Unlike Hilde's "harps in the air," the event does not defy reason; and yet, again, Solness denies it. Hilde insists, and Solness is suddenly struck by a thought: "There's some mystery behind all this—I must have thought about it. I must have willed it, wished it, longed to do it, and then—Perhaps that would explain it." Suddenly, we remember how Kaja came to be hired by the Master Builder. Once again, the exposition reveals a past shrouded in mystery, in which the concrete, historical event is dissolved in myth. The shock of this transaction is increased by combining the "impossible" and the "possible" in the myth—harps in the air and a flirtation. The "mythic" flirtation is doubly plausible because Hilde reports that Solness called the promised kingdom *Orangia*: "It sounded almost as if you were making fun of me." [66] A girl's romantic fantasy would not be likely to include a suggestion that her prince was only joking.

Now Hilde has come, on exactly the tenth anniversary of the Master Builder's promise, to claim her kingdom: "I thought to myself—if he can build the highest church tower in the world, he must surely be able to raise some sort of a kingdom as well—." [67] It is doubtful whether a real Master Builder could have raised, in Lysanger, the *highest* church tower in the world. But *the* Master

Builder, an ideal archetype, would have done precisely that, and supplied a kingdom for a girl in the bargain.

Hilde sees the Apollonian dream image of a Master Builder. This is, after all, an "illusion," visibly different from the finite, fearful man the play has thus far revealed. Yet the action has also suggested that Solness has more than natural powers, and his actions from this point on will appear in a context increasingly symbolic, increasingly mythic in its significance. Solness reveals that he has turned from the building of churches to "homes for human beings," and Hilde suggests that he add church towers to these as well: "I mean—something that soars—that points straight up into the free air—with the vane at a dizzy height!" The Master Builder has not yet explained why he ceased to build churches, and so Hilde's suggestion does not yet bear its full symbolic weight; but Solness is building a home for himself, one with a very high tower, "much too high for a home—people are sure to say!" [68] We have learned a mysterious fact which will later be clarified by further exposition—which will, in turn, open the door to a still larger mystery. It is as if every revelation in the play were a lamp which, illuminating a leaf or a face of rock in the night, served only to emphasize the encompassing darkness.

Before Mrs. Solness returns to announce dinner, the Master Builder expresses his deepest fear, and a compact is made:

SOLNESS: . . . I tell you one of these days the younger generation will thunder at my door—they'll break through and overwhelm me!

HILDE: In that case, I think that you yourself should go out and open the door to the younger generation.

SOLNESS: Open the door?

HILDE: Of course! Let them come in to you—in friendship.

SOLNESS: No, no! Don't you see? The younger generation comes bringing retribution. It heralds the turn of fortune; it marches triumphantly, under a new banner.

HILDE: (*Rises, looks at him, and says with quivering lips*): Can I be of use to you, Master Builder?

SOLNESS: You can indeed! For you too march under a new banner, it seems to me. Yes! Youth matched against youth! [69]

The ironies of this passage unveil the paradoxical nature of the play's universe. Solness is right in his obsessive, almost comic declaration that the younger generation heralds "the turn of fortune"— in the person of Hilde, it will bring him crashing to his death. Hilde, who offers to "be of use" to him, is—unlike Kaja—selfish. Yet she will help him to climb beyond fear, the past, and the younger generation.

Act Two. The second act plunges us into the abyss of truth and its terror—the background of unmediated suffering and mortal guilt from which the Master Builder, aided by Hilde, will pluck a redeeming illusion. Early in the act, Mrs. Solness tells her husband that she can never find contentment in the house he is building. Later, Hilde learns the reason, in detail, from Solness. Years ago, an old house—ugly but comfortable—stood where the new one is rising. There the Master Builder and his wife lived and had twins during the first years of their marriage. Then, there was a fire; the house burned to the ground. Everyone escaped safely, but Mrs. Solness' milk was affected by the shock, and, since she felt it was her duty to continue nursing the twins, they died. "From the day I lost them," declares Solness, "I had no joy in building churches." [70] Even the church tower in Lysanger was built without the exultant joy which Hilde had felt in witnessing its completion. Solness began to build homes for human beings. He broke the old garden into lots, and there attempted new ideas which brought success with a rush; the ashes of the old home were the foundation of his triumph as a master builder.

But that triumph as a builder was empty, a sign of what Solness had lost as a man: "In order to build these homes for others, I had to give up—give up forever—a real home of my own." The loss was not merely a personal one: "All that I have been able to achieve—everything I've built and created—all the beauty, security, comfort—magnificence, too, if you like . . . had to be paid for—not in money—but in human happiness. And I don't mean just my happiness either—but that of other people." The Master Builder's vocation in life could not be fulfilled without destroying the vocation of his wife as a mother, "building up the souls of little children." [71]

This much of the story can be understood in terms of realism; it requires no transcendental assumptions, and can be seen as a demonstration of the Newtonian—and Hegelian—principle that every action has an equal, opposite reaction. The Master Builder has learned that to destroy is to build, to build is to destroy, and suffering is the lot of the successful man as well as the failure. To the extent that the processes leading to this suffering are *impersonal*—the objective operations of a world-order—the individual is beneath both guilt and redemption.

It is at this point that the "secular" history revealed in the exposition merges with a "sacred" history beyond the horizon of historical realism. Solness believes that the fire which marked the major turning point in his life was not an accident (the event as an arbitrary collision of particles), and not an objective historical destruction of one value by another (the event as passage from Hegelian thesis to antithesis), but something *willed* by him. Long before the fire, he had noticed a crack in the chimney, and yet neglected to repair it. He began to dream of a fire which would destroy the house while his family was safely out driving in the sleigh. As it turned out, the fire began while they were at home, and in an entirely different part of the house. The *details* of the event were different, and more fraught with suffering, than what Solness had willed, but the fire had occurred. Where Naturalism might see an accident, the Master Builder sees order: "Don't you believe, Hilde, that there exist certain special, chosen people, who have been endowed with the power and faculty of . . . willing a thing, so persistently, so—inexorably—that they make it happen?" Hilde answers, cryptically: "If that is true, we'll find out some day whether *I* am one of the chosen." [72] Her will, like that of Solness, will be fulfilled at last, but with equally destructive consequences.

Either the fire was an accident, or Solness is (as he declares) to blame for the death of his children, and the instrument of his own suffering. Here Ibsen presents us with a dilemma. The play is *intelligible* only if we grant Solness the validity of his interpretation; then Hilde's appearance makes sense, as does the Master Builder's death. Otherwise, we can see only a texture of highly improbable accidents which render the play unnatural—but this negates the "realistic" approach which would lead us to reject Solness' interpretation in the first place. Yet if Solness is correct, the play's principle of intelligibility is specifically nonrational, and human action must be seen in relation to its hidden background, where the medieval God's Eternal Present reigns. It is more hidden here than it was in medieval drama, and Ibsen cannot, as did Shakespeare, bring witches onto his stage; the theater of historical man will not tolerate them. Instead, Solness *speaks about* "Helpers and Servers" who have aided him in the execution of his will.[73] The familiar spirits of witchcraft appear as the delusions of individual psychology in the ostensibly realistic universe of the play; at the same time, the play's pattern of action becomes fully intelligible only if we in some sense accept the spirits and the hidden order which they imply.

Yet Solness is a man, not a warlock, and the spirits who bring him luck bring with it a curse: "It's as though I had an open wound here on my breast; and the Helpers and Servers flay pieces of skin off other people in order to heal my wound. But it goes on burning and throbbing—it never heals—never!" Here is the Dionysiac vision of a blessing which is also a curse, like Oedipus' victory over the Sphinx. Here also the freedom of the individual affirming the *principium individuationis* is joined to an annihilation of that principle as the individual is absorbed into a universal will, like Euripides' possessed Phaedra:

HILDE: . . . something within me urged and goaded me to come here—it was as though something beckoned to me and lured me on.

SOLNESS (*Eagerly*): That's it. That's it, Hilde! There's a troll in you, just as there is in me; and it's the troll in us that summons the powers outside us; and then, whether we like it or not, we're forced to give in.[74]

Solness and Hilde will their actions, and yet are compelled to will them; free will and necessity are, here as in Euripides, coextensive.

But the Master Builder sees his will as corrupted; like the protagonist of Oedipus the King, he acknowledges his guilt. He is
chained to suffering by ideas of good and evil which Hilde rejects:
"If we had a vigorous, radiantly healthy conscience—and had the
courage to follow our own will!" Hilde affirms a robust, pre-
Christian, Viking morality, beyond good and evil. Solness will
adopt this morality, but the way in which he does so is significant.

During the dialogue, Ragnar had entered and asked the Master
Builder, without success, to write on his drawings. Now Hilde
repeats the request, and Solness refuses—again he sees the younger
generation's inevitable hand of retribution. Hilde replies:

HILDE: Don't talk like that! Do you want to kill me? Do you want
to rob me of what means more to me than life!
SOLNESS: What is that?
HILDE: The need to see you great. To see you with a wreath in
your hand—high, high up, upon a church tower! [75]

Hilde is advancing an ethic of human greatness which, if it is
above Christian morality, is also above pettiness and fear. Solness
writes on the drawings, freeing the younger generation to create,
and his new-found generosity is, paradoxically, one with the hubris
which will send him to the top of his second tower, and to his
death.

Act Three. In a dialogue with Hilde, Mrs. Solness casts new
light on the source of her husband's anguished guilt—the fire in
the old house. She also sees the death of the twins as a punishment for personal guilt—her failure to endure the misfortune of
the fire. However, her attitude toward the greater loss is different
from that of Solness: "Don't talk to me any more about the two
little boys. We must be glad for them; they are at peace and happy
now. No—it's the small losses in life that break one's heart." She
speaks of the fire's destruction of old family portraits, lace, and
above all her dolls: "I carried them under my heart. Like little
unborn children." [76] A husband grieves over his wife and children;
his wife grieves over dolls. Solness has erred in seeing in her the
equivalent of his own creative instinct; it is doubtful whether
she could ever have been a master builder of the souls of little

children. If anyone in the play is an example of abnormal psychology, it is the dull, dutiful Mrs. Solness, paralyzed by the loss of the symbols of her childhood. Her husband, on the other hand, is a man who translates personal experience into the realm of ethics and a personal confrontation with sorrow into man's confrontation with God, Who is a symbol of the contradictory ground of Being.

This universalization of the Master Builder's action and suffering is a gradual process, as we have seen. The petty individual of the opening scene has grown by degrees; now, in Act Three, Ibsen compels us to see him *sub specie aeternitatis*. Consider, for example, the expanding perspectives on his ascent of the church tower in Lysanger. Hilde's description mediated the historical event into the realm of myth; Solness denied her myth. But now Ragnar thrusts it again into its mythic context: "He's supposed to have done that once—just once in his life, they say. It's become a sort of legend among us younger men." [77]—A legend, that is, of spiritual potency now lost, and of youthful aspiration descending to the compromises of age. In this context, Solness becomes *the* Master Builder, an imitation of the eternal paradigm of man the Promethean creator who has allowed himself to be chained to the rock of quotidian experience in all its repressive finitude.

The portrait is expanded in another of the play's crucial expositions, which have cast a light of increasing intensity on the past and its mysteries. Solness tells Hilde of the churches he once built, and tells her that he built them for the honor and glory of God. God should have been pleased with his devotion, but He gave the trolls in Solness full power, and allowed the old house to burn down. The Master Builder's crucial insight into God's plan came atop the church tower at Lysanger: "I suddenly understood why He had taken my little children from me. He didn't want me to become attached to anything; I was to be allowed no love or happiness, you understand. I was to be nothing but a Master Builder, and I was to devote my life solely to building for Him." Now the moment is fully transformed into myth: Solness' climb to the church tower was a confrontation, *in illo tempore*, between the suffering worshipper and his God:

SOLNESS: Then I did the impossible. I no less than He.

HILDE: The impossible?

SOLNESS: I had never before been able to climb to a great height. But that day I did it.

HILDE: Yes, you did!

SOLNESS: And as I stood up there, high over everything, I said to Him: Listen to me, Almighty One! From now on I will be a free Master Builder; free in my sphere, just as You are in yours. I will never more build churches for You; only homes for human beings.

But the homes have been only houses, "not to be happy in," and the Master Builder's achievement has amounted to nothing. God, in short, was the victor in that first confrontation. Now there will be another, and the Master Builder will make a new promise:

SOLNESS: I believe there's just one possible dwelling place for human happiness—that's what I'm going to build now.

HILDE: Master Builder—you mean our castles-in-the-air?

SOLNESS: Castles-in-the-air, yes.

With Hilde, Solness will build, on the firm foundation of his suffering, "the loveliest thing in all the world":[78] an Apollonian realm of fair illusion above the battles of life and its God who, like the Dionysus of the *Bacchae*, demands the offering of blood from his worshippers.

The transition from the finite, secular history of the Master Builder to a sacred, anhistorical vision of his action, is nearly complete. For the greater part of the first act, we saw him as a finite man, caught up in the petty fears of quotidian existence. In the second act, he revealed the Dionysiac basis of his inaction; both he and Dionysiac man "have looked deeply into the true nature of things, they have *understood* and are now loath to act." But Hilde has helped him to overcome "the sober contemplation of actuality, the intense susceptibility to suffering, by means of illusions strenuously and zestfully entertained"—Apollonian illusions.[79] In the final scene, Apollonian illusion and Dionysiac wisdom will join in their tragic marriage.

The ascent of Solness takes place offstage, and is reported by the visible observers. There are better reasons for this than the limitations of Ibsen's physical theater: we are compelled to see the Master Builder reflected in the eyes of others, hugely, as they react with wonder to a more-than-human act, an act which everyone except Hilde regards as impossible. Ragnar has come, and he reports that the streets are full of his fellow students, the younger generation which has come to gloat while the Master Builder stays below, afraid to climb as high as he builds: "He'd get dizzy before he was halfway up. He'd have to crawl down again on his hands and knees!" But Solness does climb, and he does not turn back. He hangs the wreath on the vane:

RAGNAR: But—this is utterly impossible!

HILDE: It *is* the impossible that he's doing now. . . . Do you see anyone else up there with him?

RAGNAR: There is no one else.

HILDE: Yes—there's someone he is striving with.

RAGNAR: No—you're mistaken—

HILDE: Don't you hear a song in the air either?

RAGNAR: It must be the wind in the tree tops.

HILDE: I hear a song. A mighty song! (*Shouts with wild joyful ecstasy*) Look! Look! Now he's waving his hat! He's waving to us down here! Oh, wave—wave back to him—for now it is finished!

Yes, it is finished, consummated—the Master Builder has dared the impossible, and presented his song of triumphant defiance to the Almighty, from a church tower built on a private home, the concrete symbol of defiance. But now Hilde, who made a mortal dizzy when she waved to him from beneath an earlier tower, waves a white shawl again, and cries out his triumph; cries from the assembled crowd join hers. And the Master Builder falls, headlong, to his death. The retribution which he feared has come—it was no idle fear, but an insight into the order which governs the world—and the instrument of retribution has been the younger generation. Yet now, more than ever, the girl sings the greatness of the man she has brought down. The play ends with this exchange:

RAGNAR: What a ghastly thing. So—after all—he couldn't do it.

HILDE (*As though under a spell, with a quiet triumph*): But he climbed to the very top. And I heard harps in the air. (*Waves the shawl and cries out with wild intensity*) My—my Master Builder![80]

Hilde affirms an impossible vision. It is a moment of paradoxical triumph, like that which attends the death of King Lear. Truth and its terror are overcome by a redeeming illusion.

The triumph of the Master Builder and his fall affirm the tragic polarities of anhistoric man: the Apollonian assertion of the *principium individuationis* and its Dionysiac annihilation. In this play, Ibsen, beginning with the external conventions of realistic drama, has transcended it by revealing an ideal, mythic past through exposition, saturating the present moment with that past—which is not seen historically, but sacredly, as a series of symbolic gestures executed *in illo tempore*. We are compelled to experience the Master Builder's action and suffering, immersed in this sacred past, *sub specie aeternitatis*—as man's confrontation with God, and the confrontation between generations which will be carried on in eternal recurrence to the end of man's dominion on the earth. Solness replaced Brovik, just as Ragnar replaces Solness and will one day be replaced by a younger Master Builder. Locked within this pattern, man is eminently mortal; yet he is also, like Solness, capable of tragic greatness. He is destined to fall before the God of time, but his features are transfigured by a redeeming nobility.

The *Master Builder* demonstrates that it is possible to create, in the world of historical man, a tragic drama which touches the philosophic matrix shared by Shakespeare and the Greeks—a "valorization" of existence which involves the paradoxical wedding of the Apollonian and the Dionysiac. Solness himself draws his being from the repetition of an archetype—the ideal Master Builder, who is also, more generally, Man the autonomous creator, daring to usurp the primal function of God and inevitably crushed for his action. The Master Builder's new house is symbolic of Ibsen's achievement in this play—on the finite structure of realism, he has built a tower soaring to the heavens, probing the mystery at the hidden ground of Being. His structure is not, perhaps, the fully realized cathedral of Shakespeare's tragedies, but its tower stands, and that in itself is a wonder. It stands to the extent that Ibsen has moved his drama beyond the historical accidents of time and space, and beyond Hegel's all-embracing Reason.

·TWO MODERN PLAYWRIGHTS·

CONCLUSIONS

Shakespearean fish swam the sea, far away from land;
Romantic fish swam in nets coming to the hand;
What are all those fish that lie gasping on the strand?
                    w. b. yeats, "Three Movements"

THE triumph of Realism and Naturalism in the theater of the
nineteenth century[1] marked the ascendancy of historical man,
theoretical man, as both dramatist and the subject for drama. In
the Preface to *Thérèse Raquin*, Emile Zola speaks of Naturalism's
desire

to bring the theater into closer relation with the great movement
toward truth and experimental science which has since the last
century been on the increase in every manifestation of the human
intellect. The movement was started by the new methods of science; thence, Naturalism revolutionized criticism and history, in
submitting man and his works to a system of precise analysis, taking into account all circumstances, environment, and "organic
cases."[2]

The enterprise defined by Hegel was executed from a new viewpoint, but remained in many ways essentially the same: the actions of men were to be examined in relation to Reason. The new
Reason was, unlike that of Hegel, founded on experimental science,
and ostensibly purged of metaphysical assumptions. In this sense,
the naturalistic drama represented an "improvement" over bour-

geois tragedy and Hebbel's metaphysical historicism—that is, a closer approach to the human event as something capable of precise, unambiguous analysis through laws capable of objective verification.

But the laws of science are not laws—they are hypotheses, which can be modified or even abandoned as a science progresses. The history of science is a continual revolution, and its battlefields are strewn with the corpses of abandoned ideas. Insofar as it was "scientific," Naturalism was as mortal as the popular Darwinism on which it was based. Furthermore, it presented the theater with that most unscientific of monsters—the aesthetic artifact posing as a "slice of life."

Therefore, it is scarcely surprising that the best plays of the naturalistic movement transcended the determinate horizons marked by Zola. Gorki's *Lower Depths* is another journey into the abyss marked by Tom o'Bedlam and the Fool in *King Lear*; and Strindberg, in *The Father*, presents an obsessional vision of the man-woman relationship far removed from the dispassionate objectivity of the scientist.

Strindberg could not, in the end, remain satisfied with the limited moral and existential horizons of Naturalism, just as Ibsen could not remain satisfied with those of the realistic, "well-made" play. However, Ibsen's Realism and Strindberg's Naturalism define two visions of modern, historical man which are still being explored, usually through different formal means, by some of the most important dramatists of this century. When Ibsen's Nora slams the door and leaves the bourgeois parlor of *A Doll's House*, she is affirming something larger than a new spirit of independence in modern woman—she is proclaiming the ability of man to alter both the form and the substance of his private and social life through an autonomous historical act. Brecht's Epic Theater is, at least in theory, a Marxist version of this enterprise. Naturalism assumes a far more pessimistic stance. The protagonists of Strindberg's *Miss Julie* are locked tight within the horizons of a destiny defined by heredity and environment; they are, in the broadest sense, victims of circumstance. Naturalism sees man stripped of his creative autonomy, a grounded fish gasping on a barren strand of existence. In this sense, Beckett's *Waiting for Godot* is an outgrowth of Naturalism—a view, stripped of Darwinism, *sub specie aeternitatis*, of the absolute and narrow boundaries of human action and the folly of hope.

Alongside the "objective" viewpoints of Realism, Naturalism, and their outgrowths, we have versions of the modern drama which are "subjective" journeys into the interior of the artist's psyche— the plays of Pirandello and the German Expressionists are prime examples. But the distinction here is not quite so clear as one might hope. After all, the "objective" playwright must have some commitment to the historical or scientific hypotheses on which his drama is based—and the choice between alternate sets of hypotheses is at least partly a subjective act. On the other hand, the playwright who explores his psyche explores that which, objectively speaking, he shares with all men—and the subjective journal of his interior life is potentially an objective account of the interior life of all men. *The Master Builder* may or may not be an "autobiographical" play—what matters is that it is a universal and enduring image of human action. In the same way, Strindberg's "subjective" *Dream Play* evokes, more profoundly than the author's naturalistic drama, the whole complex scene of human action and suffering. Here the heaven, hell, and bleeding earth of a *theatrum mundi* are raised in the microcosm of the dramatist's psyche; the *I* echoes from the depths of being.

Furthermore, the "subjective" and "objective" viewpoints often fuse in unaccountable ways. The plays of Genet may be regarded as effusions of a self-absorbed, rather psychotic individual; but *The Balcony* and *The Screens* are also penetrating critiques of the rituals of society. And Bertolt Brecht's Epic dramas, intended as didactic tools of social change, often transcend the teleological optimism of Marxism, yielding to a vision of man unchanged and unchangeable by historical processes. This movement is evident in Brecht's masterpiece, *Mother Courage*.

Mother Courage: Brecht and Historical Optimism

Much critical attention has been devoted to the relation between Brecht's plays and his theoretical writings on the drama. Some writers have argued that the artist executed the intentions of the Marxist; others more numerous have played variations on Martin Esslin's contention that "the poet deep within him always had to hide behind the Marxist."[3] But what is the Marxist's version of the task of drama? In a seminal essay, "On the Experimental Theatre," Brecht declares that theater must "develop models of the social life of human beings, in order to help the spectator to understand his social surroundings and to help him control them."[4] Behind this aim lies the assumption of nineteenth-century social realism: man is capable of creating his historical destiny.

It is, therefore, hardly surprising that Brecht is uncomfortable when confronted with a work like King Lear, about which he writes:

Lear's wrath over his daughters infects the spectator, that is, the spectator, watching him, could only experience wrath, not perhaps amazement or uneasiness, and the same holds for other possible emotions. The wrath of Lear, therefore, could not be tested against its justification nor could it be provided with a prophesy of its possible consequences. It was not to be discussed, only to be shared in. In this way social phenomena appeared eternal, natural, unchangeable, unhistorical, and did not hold for discussion.[5]

In this passage, Brecht combines valid insight with an extraordinary obtuseness. Shakespeare's play is a vision of the "unchangeable, unhistorical"; but the ground of Being is the content of this vision, and not "social phenomena." More basically, there is no one-to-one correspondence between the emotions of Lear and those of the spectator; in fact, Shakespeare continually uses a highly sophisticated "alienation effect" to project us beyond the circle of Lear's individual passions—and the Fool's banter is only the most obvious of these. Perhaps Brecht fails to see this because the play's alienations do not lead to Marxist conclusions.

Brecht's theory of alienation (Verfremdung) should be understood in this context. It is a new application by historical man of a principle as old as the theater. Brecht describes *his* version in these words:

> To alienate an event or a character is simply to take what to the event or character is obvious, known, evident and produce surprise and curiosity out of it. . . . Through the technique of sympathetic understanding the actor is able to present . . . [the wrath of Lear] in such a way that the spectator . . . is in complete agreement with Lear . . . Through the technique of alienation, on the other hand, the actor presents the wrath of Lear in such a way that the spectator can be surprised at it, . . . as a social phenomenon which is not self-evident. . . . The process of alienation, then, is the process of historifying, of presenting events and persons as historical, and therefore as ephemeral.[6]

Brecht is speaking here of alienated acting, which can be employed in any dramatic work; more fundamentally, alienation is a basic aim of the dramatic devices of his Epic Theater, which modify and interrupt the dramatic illusion to destroy "sympathetic understanding" and lead the spectator to concrete thought and social action. Significantly, this is accomplished by "historifying" persons and events—assigning them an ephemeral position in a Marxist dialectic of history which transcends them.

This leads us to the aim of Epic Theater, which is to induce a process of thought and action in the spectator contributing to specific historical ends. These ends provide the "valorization" of whatever suffering the individual may undergo in attempting to achieve them. Eliade observes that "for Marxism, events are not a succession of arbitrary accidents; they exhibit a coherent structure and, above all, they lead to a definite end—final elimination of the terror of history, 'salvation.' Thus, at the end of the Marxist philosophy of history, lies the age of gold of the archaic eschatologies."[7] The historical dialectic is justified at the point where it ends—the fading away of the State under Marxism. This point resembles the triumph of the Kingdom of God which follows the Christian Second Coming. However, the Christian who is "crucified with Christ" has *already* achieved the Kingdom of God; it is present in him, a reality which transfigures his suffering. In contrast, the historical man of Marxism is a means to an end not contained within him, and which he will not witness—he is an abandoned precipitate of the chemistry of Time. His suffering is a path to history's ends, and not to fullness of being. The *principium individuationis* yields to a Marxist telos rather than Dionysiac insight and ecstasy.

Here, indeed, is a paradox: Marxism attempts to assign an autonomous value to man absent in Christianity, which referred his being to God; yet men are valuable only insofar as they serve an eschatological abstraction. The paradox is evident in Brecht's *Lehrstück* ("play for learning"), *The Mother*. Pelagea Vlassova's son has been killed as a result of his revolutionary activities, and neighbors come to comfort her. The Landlady declares: "Mankind needs God, Pelagea Vlassova. We are helpless against fate." The Mother answers: "What we say is this: the fate of man is man." Yet this "humanism" points her beyond her son, and beyond mourning, to the Cause. The Mother is a positive Marxist heroine, who rises at the end from her sickbed to carry a red flag in the vanguard of revolution, crying: "The victims of today will be victors of tomorrow." [8] Jean Genet, in *The Screens*, begins with the same affirmation, but carries it forward to the triumph of revolution, which merely serves to establish a new version of what it has overcome, a new step in a cycle of eternal recurrence. A glance at modern Communist states may suggest that Genet's insight into revolution is more "objectively" correct.

Mother Courage is a far more complex work than *The Mother*, one in which the premises of Brecht's theater are strained mightily by an art which transcends them.

Brecht writes that a performance of the play is primarily meant to show

that in wartime big business is not conducted by small people. That war is a continuation of business by other means, making the human virtues fatal even to those who exercise them. That no sacrifice is too great for the struggle against war. [9]

War, in short, is a function of Capitalism; war must be overcome, which means, in the end, that Capitalism must be overthrown.

But war makes the human virtues "fatal"—does Brecht wish to include the desire to overcome war among these virtues? Here, indeed, is a problem, to which I shall return later. For the moment, I should like to draw attention to Brecht's conscious desire that the spectator find a clear moral in the play—a desire which, oddly enough, makes him a bedfellow of Nahum Tate. Brecht's criticism of the Zurich production of 1941 casts further light on his intentions:

It sounds from press notices and spectators' reports as if the Zurich première, while attaining a high artistic level, simply presented a picture of war as a natural disaster, an unavoidable blow of fate, and so confirmed the petty-bourgeois spectator's confidence in his own indestructibility, his power of survival. Yet the play always left the equally petty-bourgeois Courage quite free to choose whether or not she should take part. Hence the production must have represented Courage's business activity, her keenness to get her cut, her willingness to take risks, as a "perfectly natural," "eternally human" way of behaving, so that she was left without any alternative.[10]

If the Zurich interpretation was doctrinally incorrect, it is as much Brecht's "fault" as that of the production. From the very beginning, Mother Courage depicts a world enveloped in war, with no clear avenue of escape. Yes, Courage voluntarily follows the troops, but her survival, and that of her children, depends on the income from the wagon.

It is only in Scene 9 that an alternative appears. The Cook offers to open an inn in Utrecht with Courage. She reacts with enthusiasm, until he tells her that it would be necessary to leave her dumb daughter behind; only then does she reject the offer. Her decision proceeds from love, not greed, and Brecht makes this consummately clear in the dialogue:

COURAGE. You mean I leave Catherine behind?
COOK. What do you think? There's no room in the inn . . . Let Catherine keep your wagon.
COURAGE. I was thinking she might find a husband in Utrecht.
COOK. With that scar? And old as she is?
COURAGE. Not so loud!

COOK. Loud or soft, what is, is. That's another reason I can't have her in the inn, the customers wouldn't like it.

COURAGE. Not so loud, I said! . . . How could she pull the wagon by herself? The war frightens her, she couldn't stand it.

At the end of the scene, Courage sees her daughter ready to leave, with her bundle, unwilling to be a hindrance. Courage assures her: "And don't think I've sent him packing on your account. It was the wagon." [11] We don't believe her. Courage has abandoned a secure business, and the arms of a lover, for her child.

From the standpoint of Brecht's avowed purpose, this was a dangerous scene to set near the end of the play. We have already seen, with relative clarity, how Courage's sons have died because of her involvement in the war; even Catherine's dumbness is a result of it. The sergeant who recruits Eilif in the first scene answers her protests in these words: "Your brood should get fat off the war, and the poor war shouldn't ask a thing in return; it can look after itself, huh?" [12] The war giveth, but the war also taketh away, and those who profit from the war shall be consumed by it. The lesson is a clear one.

In Scene 3, Swiss Cheese is executed because Courage haggles too long over the amount of a bribe. Again, the lesson seems clear-cut. Yet even here there are complications. The bribe would have financially wrecked Courage, leaving both her and her daughter without a source of livelihood. Furthermore, Swiss Cheese has been captured because he lacks the very qualities that lead Courage to haggle. This obscures Brecht's didactic point, and suggests a fatalistic view of human action which, whatever its ethical content, leads to the destruction of the individual. One thing only is clear: war is a dialectic of destruction, which consumes ethical opposites with equal savagery. How, then, are we to get beyond war?

When a temporary peace finally comes, Courage cries out against it, since it will be bad for business. It is also bad for Eilif, who is arrested and destined to be executed for an act which won him praise as a hero during the fighting. In a sense, then, peace is as destructive to Courage's children as war. In isolation, this may be a rather perverse interpretation of the action; but it is supported by

Scene 10, where the Cook offers Courage an exit from the war which would require her to abandon one of her children—and Brecht has made the fate of those children the most important argument *against* the war. Had Courage abandoned Catherine for a peaceful trade, she would have betrayed the very thing which makes her participation in the war reprehensible and absurd. In Scene 10, the critical process which the "alienated" spectator is supposed to bring to the play encounters a tragic paradox, and its meaning for man is formulated by the Dionysiac insight of Silenus rather than dialectical materialism.

The last two scenes of *Mother Courage* serve merely to sharpen the paradox. Like a true positive heroine, Catherine lifts her tattered banner against war—the drum with which she warns the town of Halle of impending invasion. Yet her reasons for lifting the banner are, unlike those of Vlassova in *The Mother*, "irrational": she loves children, and cannot bear the thought that they will be slaughtered by the invading army. She saves the town, but is herself destroyed. She might have been saved, as the Peasants point out, if Courage hadn't gone off to the town to get her "cut," leaving Catherine behind. But how does the alienation effect work here? If we regard the actions of Catherine and her mother critically, we are forced to conclude that the drums should *not* have been beaten, and the town left to its destruction. On the other hand, Brecht declares that the play should show "that no sacrifice is too great for the struggle against war." Only the "sympathetic understanding" which he deplores will lead us, in the context of Catherine's action, to accept this conclusion. The town is saved, but Catherine dies, and the war—in spite of her—continues. Rationally, it is impossible to avoid the thought that the townsmen who were spared along with their children might, as soldiers, slaughter children in the towns of their invaders.

In *Mother Courage*, Brecht transcends the circuit of a Marxist didacticism with an anhistorical vision of man and his relation to war, a bitter and yet compassionate view of the "eternally human." If war stands condemned, it is not at all clear how man may develop "historically" beyond it. Mother Courage *could* raise her banner in the end, like Pelagea Vlassova, but Catherine's end affirms the objective futility of the action, and we have, at last, only Courage's incredible capacity to endure. The closing lines of her final song convey both the glory and the bitterness of that human endurance in the teeth of suffering:[13]

> The spring is here, get out of bed
> The snow melts fast, green buds arrive
> You'll sleep forever when you're dead
> But if you're not, then look alive!

The Screens: The Problem of Being

Brecht achieves an anhistorical view of man in spite of the rational, historicist assumptions of his own Marxism. Genet, on the other hand, *begins* with an anhistorical viewpoint. In *The Screens*, he shows that individuals and states cannot create an autonomous meaning for their existence, a meaning which transcends the rituals and values of the historical past.

Much contemporary drama is built upon the Nietzschean premise: God is dead. The consequences are, for each playwright, inevitable, though that inevitability assumes different shapes. The works of Beckett, Ionesco, Pinter are half-inarticulate cries at the edge of an abyss whose name is Absence, and the Absence implies its necessary but unattainable opposite. It implies the Presence which *was*, which preceded it either historically or as an existential predicate, therefore the Presence which existed or may come to exist as Being, and which exists now as idea only, as the logical negation of a negative immediately experienced. Immediacy is, for these playwrights, despair; yet it is a sentimental despair, it implies a time of fullness of Being which it can never attain, but without whose metaphysical presence it cannot take shape. Vladimar and Estragon wait for a Godot which is "the good old days," whether its existence is temporal past or future or the imagined shape of either; and so, though they have no proper history, despair manifests itself to them historically and with that yearning which we sometimes call sentimentality. The writers of what Martin Esslin calls "the Theatre of the Absurd"[14] strive for new ideas, and find themselves embroiled in old attitudes (however well disguised); they strive for new forms, and find instead the shape of an old dilemma.

Genet is both more conservative and more radical than these dramatists. For him as for Christianity, Presence, positive Being, exists now. It is not the Absence of Godot which supplies Genet's existential predicament, but rather His pervasive Presence. Not insufficient Being, but Being so absolute it negates isolation, surrounds, oppresses. The dilemma of man for Genet is not in his loneliness, but rather the fact that *he is not lonely enough.*

The problem of Being is inextricably tied to that of doing, as Jean-Paul Sartre observes in his ontological biography, *Saint Genet:*

Action, whatever it be, modifies that which is in the name of that which is not yet. Since it cannot be carried out without breaking up the old order, it is a permanent revolution. It demolishes in order to build and disassembles in order to reassemble. . . . Our unstable societies fear lest a false movement cause them to lose their balance. They therefore ignore the negative moment of our activities. . . . The right-thinking man castrates himself; he cuts the negative moment away from his freedom and casts out the bloody mess. Freedom is thus cut in two; each of its halves wilts away separately. One of them remains within us. It identifies forever Good with Being, hence with what already is.

The Good of historical man is identified with this conception of Being, an orderly sum of "customs and tradition," and Evil is Other than Being:

But as . . . we have forged its concept by dividing that which was not divisible and by separating with a single stroke the two indivisible moments of human freedom, we are forced to recognize that Good and Evil are rigorously contemporary, that is, in religious language, they are two equally immortal principles. . . . By Evil one therefore means both the Being of Nonbeing and the Nonbeing of Being.[15]

A writer like Beckett places us in a position beyond Good and Evil while displaying an inverted dependence on these categories. Genet accepts the categories and (as we shall discover) transcends them from within. It is in this sense that his art is at once revolutionary and conservative.

The process is illustrated in Saïd, whose dramatic evolution is the center of the complex patterns of development of *The Screens*. Saïd begins and ends as an outcast, yet the spiritual distance he travels from the beginning of the play to its end is enormous. At first, Saïd (and his mother) squat at the bottom of an already low Algerian society. Even among the Arabs, their poverty is extreme; and the poverty of Saïd is matched to the ugliness of his bride-to-be, Leila. Saïd's mother observes: "She's left over because she's ugly. And you, because you're poor. She needs a husband, you a wife. She and you take what's left, you take each other." [16] These words define both their alienation and its incompleteness; having nothing but each other, they still have that; and their marriage, however bitter, places them within the pale of social relations, gives them a title (however slight) to Being.

Or so it appears, deceptively. For Saïd, his mother, and Leila can appropriate Being only to the extent that it is accessible to the Arabs. But the Arabs are slaves to the colonizers, and therefore partake (passively) of Nonbeing. They are the Other of Sir Harold and his lot, and therefore (in Sartre's terminology) Evil. But their Evil has not reached its self-conscious stage, and their Being is illusion.

Having neither Being nor its pure opposite, Saïd and the two women radicalize their alienation; they become thieves. When the mother attempts to mourn a corpse with the village women, one of them expresses the Arab illusion: "You're a family of thieves. Here in the village we have a right to dispense our own justice. We're among ourselves. You won't follow the corpse." Justice among the Arabs? We are reminded of Solange's words in *The Maids*: "When slaves love one another, it's not love." [17] When slaves dispense justice, it's not justice, and that is their dilemma.

The situation is radicalized by the Arab revolt. The revolt can exist only insofar as the revolutionaries recognize their Nonbeing, internalize the Evil which negates the Good of the right-thinking man, the colonizer, and take on the negative moment of freedom.

But in doing so they imitate Saïd, the most perfect example of Nonbeing among them, Saïd the outcast and the criminal. Kadidja, the village woman who spoke of Arab "justice," now speaks of something else:

Saïd, Leila, my loved ones! You, too, in the evening related the day's evil to each other. You realized that in evil lay the only hope. Evil, wonderful evil, you who remain when all goes to pot, miraculous evil, you're going to help us. I beg of you, evil, and I beg you standing upright, impregnate my people. And let them not be idle! [18]

The desire for Evil is absolute, and, for a while, the Arabs revel in it, drunk with rape and fire, with lies and butcheries. They learn of Saïd; they achieve the Being of Nonbeing.

Yet now the pendulum swings the other way. The Arabs gradually become noble. They must become noble, it is a necessity even to their enemy, the French Lieutenant:

gentlemen, behind those hills it's men you'll have to gut, not rats. But the Arabs are rats. For a split second, in the hand-to-hand fighting, take a good look at them—if they give you time—and discover, but fast, the humanity that's in them. Otherwise, you'd be killing rats, and you'd have waged war and made love only with rats.[19]

The Arabs learn to wear uniforms, they acquire discipline, they march, they die heroically. An old woman, Ommu, chastises one of them:

go join the other side where there's stately beauty, you little snotnose! But maybe you've done it, you're joining them, and copying them excites you. To be their reflection is already to be one of them: forehead to forehead, nose to nose, chin to chin, belly to belly [20]

Gradually, the Arabs are becoming less Evil. As Sartre observes: "If Evil wants to become absolute, it must be an object of loathing to the one who commits it. If the evil man could be in harmony with himself, this harmony would have the appearance of Good." [21] For the Arabs, this harmony is more than the appearance of Good; it is Good itself. They have begun to appropriate Being to themselves; having negated their oppressors, the good men, the righteous colonizers, they now become them.

For the Arabs, Evil has been an action not brought to completion; but Saïd strives to complete it. Leila strives also, but less successfully; and Saïd's mother fails, despite herself. Her chief shame among the dead is the fact that she has accidentally killed a French soldier, and is acclaimed by the Arabs as a heroine. But Saïd is a traitor. He does not will Evil to the French for the Good of the Arabs; he wills Evil absolutely. He has chosen and continues to choose the negative moment of freedom, the opposite of Being in any of its forms. When the Nonbeing of the Arabs becomes Being, he is the negation of that Being. Since his action is this immortal principle, there is a mythic dimension to his existence, he is larger than life. Habib says of him:

What about your sighing? Eh? Your sighing? You yawned so much that you swallowed all the birds and there were none left to eat the plant lice. The vines suffered because of your sighing.

And large words choir his final entrance on the stage:

Make way for him. Push aside. Push aside the houses and gardens too. And the whole town if necessary to receive the native son in state! Push aside the night . . . push back the wheels of the planets to the edge of the wheel of heaven . . . and let them fall into the void to clear the way for us![22]

The final extension of Saïd is a disruption of the order of the cosmos, the absolute negation of absolute Being which is, at the same time, necessary to Being, just as Satan is necessary to God. This is a consequence suggested, if not elaborated in the play. Yet Saïd the doer, the man of action, is not quite our mythic principle. His particular evils have been minor: "As regards betrayal, you did what you could, and there we're obliged to say that you didn't achieve much." Therefore his stature in Evil must be measured by what he has achieved less directly:

Saïd, if we were able to sustain our frenzy to the bitter end, or almost, heedless of the gazes that were judging us, it was because we had the luck to have you—not as a model, no, not as a model! . . . As a flag.[23]

He has been a flag, a banner to the Arabs in their pursuit of Evil; but the end of their Evil was Being, and therefore Good. Saïd, at the end of the play, discovers his Nonbeing posited as Being.

If the tragedy of the Good man lies in his inability to cut away the negative moment from his freedom, the tragedy of the Evil man, of Saïd, lies in his inability to cut away the positive moment from that freedom. Unwittingly, his denial is transformed into an affirmation.

Saïd the living thief is Evil, and therefore dangerous to the new Being which the Arabs have created for themselves. But Saïd the dead thief can be a living banner (equivalent, perhaps, to the Joan of Lorraine of the French), a saint, most useful when his presence is symbolic and given the shape of Being. Saïd is offered immortality: "Your brow in the nebulae and your feet in the ocean . . . And standing till the end of time." Resolute in his affirmation of Nonbeing, he rejects the offer: "To the old gal, to the soldiers, to all of you, I say shit." His statement is a particular negation, but circumstances create a different grammar for his destiny. Saïd is tempted, and Saïd is trapped. His temptation lies in this recognition: "I'm very much in demand. I can set my price." The first temptation of Evil is a price, the possibility of a reward, an end for Evil outside Evil, which makes it a Good. Saïd's mother cries out against this from the world of the dead:

Saïd! . . . you're not going to give in? She-dog that I am, she-dog big with a mongrel pup, I kept you in my guts not to become one more one less! . . . Don't let yourself be conned by either the old girl or the soldiers. Don't serve either of them, don't serve any purpose whatever. I think they're going to make up a song about you. The words have been written. People are humming it. It's in the air. (*She screams.*) Saïd, squelch the inspiration, shit on them! [24]

Saïd in fact overcomes temptation; he turns his back on the Arabs, leaves, and is shot.

But the trap is unavoidable. If Saïd's Nonbeing needed a Being to which it could be opposed, an inevitable consequence of his Evil was the Arab Good. In the last lines of the play, the mother asks, "Where is he? In a song?" [25] For us, the question becomes a statement of fact. Saïd's song is the play itself.

Only when the play stands before as a play, as song rather than fact, is the final paradox of Evil revealed. Genet affirms Nonbeing; he posits the negative moment of freedom. But the form of this postulation is a song, a play, a work of art. We, the right-thinking men whose realm is Being, admit his song to the realm of Being, transform it into a Good. Or rather, we restore the positive moment to that act of freedom which is the song itself. But if Genet is tricked in this way, so are we; we are compelled to admit the negative with the positive moment of freedom, and Evil is enthroned in our consciousness along with Good.

The Being against which Saïd rebels is identical, as Sartre observes, with "customs and tradition." [26] This modern version of nomos is a creation of *historical* man: Being is seen as an expression of a post-Hegelian Reason, purged of the irrational and the daemonic, essentially Good. Historical man has banished the Furies from the state. Genet, like Aeschylus, realizes that they cannot be banished. Saïd and the Algerian rebels of *The Screens* unleash the Furies against the nomos of the French. But if Being cannot exist without Nonbeing, Nonbeing cannot exist without Being, and Evil is finally absorbed in the Good. The wheel has turned full circle. Revolution and the process of historical progress which it implies for the Marxist is seen as merely a transition to a new version of the old order, a step in the anhistorical process of eternal recurrence.

In this process, the *principium individuationis* is shattered. Saïd cannot create an historically autonomous meaning for his existence. He becomes a banner for the new Being of the Arabs, a song, a mythic archetype of the Evil at the basis of their Good. If he is not a tragic hero, caught in the eternal rhythm of suffering, he is nevertheless a figure symbolic of the darkness at the core of the luminous state—a darkness which, like that of the Furies at the end of the *Eumenides*, has been tamed by the need for order and set apart in a symbolic grove.

Genet's drama is a new version of Dionysiac art. The enterprise of historical man from the time of Hegel has been to eliminate the negative moment of action by subordinating it to some version of Reason, the vision of an intelligible universe. Even the Marxist vision of the class struggle, founded on contradictions in the social order, subversive of bourgeois tradition, is a continuation of this enterprise, looking forward to the moment when history will be consummated and the rational order of the working class stand triumphant. But Genet sees the *eternal* contradiction in Being, which necessarily posits Nonbeing; and this is a Dionysiac insight.

Like the *Bacchae* and *King Lear*, unlike most of the fragmented accomplishment of modern drama, *The Screens* presents a total vision of human action, a vision without compromise. Genet has brought us to the farthest limits of man's freedom, and we return purged by fire and deeply aware of our possibilities for the terrible and the sublime. The drama cannot do much more.

Considerations: History and the Tragic Vision

"Basic to the tragic form," says Richard Sewall, "is its recognition of the inevitability of paradox, of unresolved tensions and ambiguities, of opposites in precarious balance. Like the arch, tragedy never rests." [27] This is an insight confirmed by the plays considered in this study. What emerges most strongly is a sense of the turbulence of the tragic experience, and its affirmation of a cosmos whose coherence is experienced as a paradox, a cosmos inevitably bound to chaos. The joint rule of Athene and the Furies over Athens is one version of the paradox; Lear's final, transfigured vision is another, both more personal and more extreme.

The tragic paradox reveals a profoundly dualistic world, and the most characteristic habit of thought of Western philosophy since Plato has been (as William Barrett observes [28]) its dualism. However, there has usually been one significant difference between our philosophic (and religious) tradition and the tragic vision. The former tends to separate earthly existence from some version of transcendence which is more unified, more perfect, more absolute in value—Plato's Ideas, Hegel's Spirit, the God of Christianity. Most of the tragedies here considered present another vision: the ground of Being is itself contradictory, and human action and suffering both reflect and paradoxically resolve its contradictions. Reduced to its simplest terms, this means: what is right and wrong about man is not peculiar to him, but rather *inherent* in the universal order of things. The ultimate "archetype" which tragic man imitates is the ground of Being itself, which manifests its eternal contradictions under the guise of a myth, a religion, a philosophy.

Western philosophy and religion has tended, on the whole, to perceive that which entails a contradiction as deficient in Being, and so has assigned the contradictory to Creation rather than the god or principle which is its source. In this manner, Plato sees the "real world," the world perceived by the senses, as composite, defective; St. Augustine is compelled to discuss Evil as the Nonbeing of Good to preserve God's perfection; and Hegel sees the contradictions of history as a means to the final unity of Spirit. From the standpoint of suffering man, these divisions are, at best, abstract—removed from the concretely apprehended sphere of his torments. He experiences *both* poles of a contradiction with equal substantiality, while referring each to a real, if hidden source. Since the drama operates in this concrete realm, it is peculiarly suited to convey the texture and substance of his experience. Even the medieval mysteries, in spite of St. Augustine, made Heaven and Hell-mouth equally real locations on their *theatrum mundi*.

In tragedy, the contradictions are felt with a particular intensity. Here we are at the keystone of the arch of which Sewall speaks, and two unstable torrents of stone rise and press upon it, achieving a paradoxical stability in their very opposition, a stability which depends upon the keystone. In the *Oresteia*, the half-arches manifest themselves as Apollo and the Furies; in *King Lear*, they are good and evil. But the simile is not entirely accurate: the arch is static; tragedy, and the tensions which inform it, dynamic—they find the necessary balance.

Tragedy provides a rehearsal of the contradictions in the ground of Being as they relate to man, concretely. These contradictions manifest themselves in a variety of ways, assume different names in different plays when they are named at all. Apollo and the Furies in the *Oresteia*, and Aphrodite and Artemis in *Hippolytus*, are merely two sets of dramatic masks which they wear. Anhistorical tragedy sees the contradictions themselves as permanent, eternal, and therefore outside time. Dionysiac perception is the apprehension of these contradictions as they are expressed in nature and man; it probes into what Lorca calls "the dark root of a scream." [29] Apollonian illusion is the transmutation of that scream into a song, a tragic song: it hears the harps in the air which surround the Master Builder's plunge. Both the dark root's scream and its song are eternally real—the simultaneous moments to which each tragedy converges by its independent path. The authors who have produced tragedies in this sense stand at historically isolated points on the rim of a wheel, sending radii to a common center outside history.

Historical tragedy, on the other hand, displays a primary awareness of the wheel itself, of pure temporality. Or rather, it sees a straight road instead of a wheel—the linear path of history, to which the recurrent mortal cycles of birth and death must accommodate themselves as best they can. For a Hegel, the primary fact about a man is that he acts at a particular moment in history; for anhistorical tragedy, the primary fact is that he acts and suffers as other men have acted and suffered, not *then* but, *sub specie aeternitatis, now*. There is a very fundamental sense in which Lear and Oedipus are contemporaries. Earlier, I discussed the different historical situations of Aeschylus and Euripides, a difference which led to contrasting styles, contrasting formulations of the contradictions in the ground of Being and the possibilities for their resolution. But this is the point at which they converge, the common tragic perception outside history. Both playwrights are able, in Nietzsche's words, "to give to quotidian experience the stamp of the eternal." And what binds *The Master Builder* or *King Lear* to *Oedipus* is a "profound, if unconscious, conviction of the relativity of time and the metaphysical meaning of life." [30] That metaphysical meaning is not an abstraction; it is the content of a radical experience. The tragic hero's initiation into the metaphysics of Being is a baptism by fire.

Yet I have been speaking primarily of a certain kind of tragedy, whose assumptions are not those of historical man. This displays, of course, a certain prejudice on my part—a preference for Dionysiac rather than rational art, a hunger for the paradoxical affirmation, a discontent with abstraction which expresses itself in abstract terms. The question remains: What is the essential distinction between the anhistorical and the historical vision of the tragic? Perhaps the question can best be answered by looking again at King Lear, which can be seen in terms of both visions, containing them, as it were, at their point of ultimate stress.

The ground bass is quotidian experience. Men act, suffer, laugh, die. A secular sun rises; rain falls; the chambers of time are filled now with the clamor of swords or leaves, now with silence. A messenger comes to the palace, another departs. This secular progression, flow, change, is common to all tragedy, indeed to all drama. But what does it mean? Beneath the accidental event, the seemingly spontaneous gesture, there is a pattern; even random motion, the Brownian Motion of physics, obeys definite laws. What is the nature of the pattern displayed by the visible surface of quotidian experience?

Historical man has his answers, answers which depend on any of a number of theoretical positions. Looking at Lear, the Hegelian would declare: "The true course of dramatic development consists in the annulment of contradictions viewed as such, in the reconciliation of the forces of human action, which alternately strive to negate each other in their conflict."[31] The reconciliation is in the realm of Reason, and defines a particular moment in the progress of Universal History. Or (as with Hebbel): the individual opposes the Idea and is crushed; there is no reconciliation.

The Darwinian advocate of naturalism would search into Lear, Cordelia, Goneril, for "the mechanism of the phenomena inherent in man, . . . the machinery of his intellectual and sensory manifestations, under the influence of heredity and environment," ready to conclude that "a like determinism will govern the stones of the roadway and the brain of man." [32] The characters are parties in a mechanically determined struggle for existence. But whom does natural selection select, amid the human debris of the stage?

The Marxist would probe the historical necessities of class struggle. How many peasants have fallen in the war? Or, more profoundly: Lear descends to a vision of unaccommodated man; madness is not the answer to his vision, but the understanding that the lot of unaccommodated man must be improved by the fall of all kings.

There are, of course, other possible historical approaches to the play, as numerous as the available modern orthodoxies. Of chief interest here are the approaches which have been most influential in the formation of modern drama—the various versions of a Hegelian idealism on the one hand, and on the other, the assorted brands of materialism. But Hegel today seems rather old-fashioned, stuffy, Spirit-ridden, and his chief influence on life as it is lived has been through Marx, who advances an historical *materialism* with close affinities to Darwin. "Now that the Idea itself has vanished," observes Gilson, "Hegel's dialectic must be understood as the law of the evolution of matter in time, and of all the biological and social phenomena rooted in matter and determined by it." [33]

In this perspective, *King Lear* becomes a demonstration of the failure of metaphysics in a deterministic universe. The characters who call upon some transcendent principle are not answered. Lear's cries are absorbed in the void; he is denied even *malevolent* gods. Or rather, Lear's material cries echo against recalcitrant matter, the heedless stones of the world. His madness is not a path to insight and redemption, but a version of the organism's decay. His search for a metaphysical meaning to his fate is grotesque, ugly, the howl of an extinct beast in the graveyards of history.

But materialism has its optimistic as well as its pessimistic phase, its positive as well as its negative moment. In positing a materially determined universe, it also advances the claim that man, through his science of matter, may control matter and exhibit its intelligibility. The world is translucent to reason and (in time) it will become transparent. Nature, like the sovereign Lear, grants its children the weapon by which it may be overcome. Yet, as Albany observes, the offspring "which contemns its origin/Cannot be bordered certain in itself" (IV, ii, 38–39). Beneath scientific reason gapes the abyss of the irrational—not Dionysiac ecstasy, but the finger which presses the button releasing the thermonuclear bomb. The Furies which have been denied a place in the modern dispensation enter with a vengeance, and in disguise.

Modern reason is, in fact, an extreme far removed from Apollonian moderation. It is not an expression of the *principium individuationis*, but a means to the systematic control of individuals in the name of fascism, communism, democracy, and, finally, in the name of science.

The modern, theoretical man of *King Lear* is Edmund. He is free from superstition, a "scientist" who learns the laws of life from a nature devoted to the survival of the fittest. From the standpoint of scientific materialism, he should emerge triumphant at the end; and yet he falls. Here the positive moment of materialism is abrogated; we are left with only its negative determinism. The final extension of the historical vision of tragedy is the collision of particles in a void. Life is emptied of its metaphysical content, and yet, paradoxically, it becomes more abstract, the expression of a scientific equation. But the metaphysical probings of anhistorical tragedy are an expression of the *concrete immediacy* of human suffering. Tragic man, aware of both the value and the limitations of his individual being, penetrates the veil of quotidian experience to a vision of the tragic ground of Being, torn by contradictions. At the point of contradiction, the dark root of the scream, his song which is also the song of Being rises, triumphant, like the musical clamor of crossed swords. That music cannot be separated from the battle itself, and tragic man stands " 'twixt two extremes of passion, joy and grief" (V, ii, 234).

It is, at last, impossible to speak of a tragic "valorization" of human existence in the context of modern scientific historicism. If the fallen hero is an abandoned step in an evolutionary process, or a particle in a chance collision, his existence has, properly speaking, no value. This is the negative moment of materialism. If, on the other hand, the hero contributes to an historical end—like Pavel in *The Mother*—his existence has a value only outside himself, and his suffering and death are merely personal by-products of social activity. The positive moment of materialism stands "beyond" tragedy.

Both moments are bounded by scientific reason and the assumption of an intelligible material world with no mysterious transhistorical significance. But modern science has already reached what Nietzsche prophetically called "those outer limits where the optimism implicit in its logic must collapse." [34] Heisenberg's Principle of Indeterminacy demonstrates the essential limits of our capacity to know and predict the behavior of the material world; and Kurt Gödel has demonstrated that mathematics, traditionally the supreme model of rationality and intelligibility, contains insoluble problems that will forever prevent its formalization in any complete system. Modern man has peeled the onion of reason only to discover that it has no center, and history, in all its tortuous unfolding, will not bring science to the bottom of the abyss of Being. Historical tragedy is, in this context, already outmoded. Its assumption that the world is rationally intelligible, stripped of mystery, has been called into question by the activity which once gave it most support. Historicism collapses as an inevitable result of the history of science. Hebbel and Zola and the theory (not always the drama) of Brecht recede into a dusty past. Once again, the more than rational rhythms of tragedy—tragedy in the old sense—are possible for man. Yet they have always in a sense been possible—the Ibsen of *The Master Builder* did not require a license from Gödel for his confrontation with the mystery of Being.

Tragedy always *begins* with quotidian life, with history experienced concretely, not in terms of a systematic science or philosophy, but then moves beyond that experience. It sees the universal contradictions in the ground of Being behind the particular contradictions of the world and the heart of man; and it celebrates both; they are of one substance; the mystery of Being is also the mystery of man. Like human suffering, that mystery is eternal. Tragedy unites man with man, and both with the sacred context of their suffering, in the flood of Dionysiac perception. Yet the suffering remains at the same time individual, bounded; under Apollo's sun, Hamlet is not Oedipus. Tragic man imitates eternal archetypes—a passion or rhythm of action with a sacred meaning, the Aphrodite of Phaedra or Lear's pattern of "Christian" redemption—yet he also transcends the archetype in his concrete particularity. And quotidian experience, secular reality, remains a fact of the tragic vision, the source of its necessary paradox. It must always see the corpse of Cordelia as well as the sacred breath on her lips.

Tragic man, a funambulist in thought and action, walks the dizzy path between quotidian life and the eternity of Being, between the two meanings of his single passion. As he plunges headlong to the ground, he may fail to see the metaphysical net which makes his destruction meaningful, or see redemption in the eternal recurrence of his anguished cry. Here "history" is manifest, the moment irredeemable; but the Chinamen of Yeats' "Lapis Lazuli," who are in one sense a symbol for the transforming power of tragic art, sit with glittering, gay eyes above the scene, and play their mournful melodies. The funambulist and their song are inseparable; without the song, his cry is merely another sound in the night; and the song could not exist without his blood.

NOTES, BIBLIOGRAPHY, AND INDEX

· NOTES ·

Introduction: Tragedy and History

1. William Butler Yeats, "Lapis Lazuli," *The Collected Poems of W. B. Yeats* (New York: Macmillan, 1956), pp. 291–93.
2. Mircea Eliade, *Cosmos and History: The Myth of the Eternal Return*, trans. Willard R. Trask (New York: Harper, 1959).
3. *Ibid.*, p. xi.
4. *Ibid.*, p. 4.
5. *Ibid.*, p. xi.
6. *Ibid.*, p. 88.
7. *Ibid.*, p. 89.
8. *Ibid.*, p. 44.
9. See for example, Richard Schechner, "Approaches to Theory/Criticism," *Tulane Drama Review*, X, No. 4 (Summer, 1966), 20–28.
10. Eliade, *op. cit.*, p. xi.
11. Friedrich Nietzsche, *The Birth of Tragedy and the Genealogy of Morals*, trans. Francis Golffing (Garden City, N.Y.: Doubleday, 1956), pp. 19, 20, 21.
12. *Ibid.*, p. 22.
13. Dagobert D. Runes, ed., *Dictionary of Philosophy* (Paterson, N.J.: Littlefield, 1964), p. 250.
14. Nietzsche, *op. cit.*, p. 22.
15. *Ibid.*, p. 23.
16. *Ibid.*
17. *Ibid.*, pp. 51, 27, 27, respectively.

18. *Ibid.*, p. 30.
19. *Ibid.*, p. 29.
20. *Ibid.*, p. 19.
21. *Ibid.*, pp. 51, 119, 13, respectively.
22. *Ibid.*, p. 56.
23. *Ibid.*, p. 53.
24. Eliade, *op. cit.*, p. 3.
25. Eliade, *op. cit.*, p. 85.
26. Nietzsche, *op. cit.*, pp. 32–33.
27. Plato, *The Republic*, trans. Paul Shorey, in Edith Hamilton & Huntington Cairns, eds., *The Collected Dialogues of Plato, Including the Letters* (New York: Pantheon, 1963), p. 748.
28. *Ibid.*, pp. 822–23.
29. Nietzsche, *op. cit.*, p. 142.
30. *Ibid.*, p. 139.
31. Eliade, *op. cit.*, p. 152.
32. Nietzsche, *op. cit.*, p. 142; Eliade, *op cit.*, pp. 139–62 passim.
33. Nietzsche, *op. cit.*, pp. 25–26.
34. *Ibid.*, p. 79.
35. *Ibid.*, p. 10.

The Oresteia

1. The quotation is from Arrowsmith's "The Criticism of Greek Tragedy," *Tulane Drama Review*, III, No. 3 (Spring, 1959), 34.
2. Norman J. DeWitt, "The Ars Poetica of Horace," *Drama Survey*, I, No. 2 (Fall, 1961), 151.

3. Friedrich Nietzsche, *The Birth of Tragedy and the Genealogy of Morals*, p. 57.

4. *Ibid.*, p. 58.

5. *Ibid.*, p. 56.

6. *Ibid.*, pp. 58, 59.

7. Translations of *Agamemnon, The Libation Bearers*, and *The Eumenides* used in this chapter are by Richmond Lattimore, and may be found in David Grene & Richmond Lattimore, eds., *Aeschylus, I* (New York: Modern Library, n.d.).

8. Nietzsche, *op. cit.*, p. 60.

9. Mircea Eliade, *Cosmos and History: The Myth of the Eternal Return*, p. 4.

10. Arrowsmith, "The Criticism of Greek Tragedy," p. 49.

11. Nietzsche, *op. cit.*, p. 97.

12. *Ibid.*, p. 11.

13. Eliade, *op. cit.*, p. 88.

The Grove of the Furies

1. Friedrich Nietzsche, *The Birth of Tragedy and the Genealogy of Morals*, pp. 89, 106.

2. *Ibid.*, p. 81.

3. J. B. Bury, *A History of Greece to the Death of Alexander the Great* (New York: Modern Library, 1937), pp. 374, 489.

4. W. B. Yeats, "From the 'Antigone,'" *The Collected Poems of W. B. Yeats* (New York: Macmillan, 1956), p. 272.

5. Thucydides, *The Peloponnesian War*, trans. Rex Warner (Baltimore: Penguin Books, 1954), p. 208.

6. *Philoctetes*, ll. 50–100. Translators of passages from Greek tragedy quoted here are David Grene (*Oedipus the King, Philoctetes, Hippolytus*), Robert Fitzgerald (*Oedipus at Colonus*), William Arrowsmith (*Heracles, The Bacchae*), and Richmond Lattimore (*The Eumenides*). All in David Grene & Richmond Lattimore, eds., *The Complete Greek Tragedies*, Vols. I–VII (New York: Modern Library, n.d.).

7. Thucydides, *op. cit.*, p. 209.

8. *Ibid.*, p. 210.

9. David Grene & Richmond Lattimore, eds., *Greek Tragedies* (Chicago: University of Chicago Press (Phoenix), 1960), Vol. I, p. 108; Vol. III, p. 109.

10. *Oedipus at Colonus*. See n. 6.

11. Nietzsche, *op. cit.*, pp. 26, 27.

12. William Arrowsmith, "A Greek Theatre of Ideas," *Arion*, II, No. 3 (Autumn, 1963), 36.

13. *Ibid.*, *passim*; E. R. Dodds, *The Greeks and the Irrational* (Berkeley: University of California Press, 1956), p. 187.

14. Arrowsmith, "A Greek Theatre of Ideas," p. 40.

15. *Ibid.*

16. Dodds, *op. cit.*, p. 186.

17. Arrowsmith, "A Greek Theatre of Ideas," p. 40.

18. *Oedipus the King* (see n. 6), ll. 895–96.

19. *Heracles* (see n. 6), l. 1424.

20. Nietzsche, *op. cit.*, p. 57.

21. Mircea Eliade, *Cosmos and History: The Myth of the Eternal Return*, p. 12.

22. *Ibid.*, p. xi.

23. Arrowsmith, "A Greek Theatre of Ideas," pp. 41, 34.

24. Dodds, *op. cit.*, pp. 182–83.

25. Nietzsche, *op. cit.*, p. 79.

26. *Ibid.*, pp. 58–59, 66–67.

27. *Ibid.*, p. 57.

28. Eliade, *op. cit.*, p. 12.

29. Dodds, *op. cit.*, p. 31.

30. Aristotle, *The Poetics*, in *Aristotle's Theory of Poetry and Fine Art.* 4th ed., ed. & trans. by S. H. Butcher (New York: Dover, 1951), p. 47 (XIII, 6).

The Tragic Universe of *King Lear*

1. Sylvan Barnet, "Some Limitations of a Christian Approach to Shakespeare," in Laurence Michel & Richard B. Sewall, eds., *Tragedy: Modern Essays in Criticism* (Englewood Cliffs, N.J.: Prentice-Hall, 1963), p. 200.

2. H. D. F. Kitto, *Form and Meaning in Drama: A Study of Six Greek Plays and of Hamlet* (New York: University Paperbacks, 1960), p. 222.

3. *Ibid.*, pp. 222, 223.

4. John Dennis Hurrell, "The Figural Approach to Medieval Drama," *College English*, XXVI, No. 8 (May, 1965), 588–604.

5. Erich Auerbach, *Scenes from the Drama of European Literature: Six Essays* (New York: Meridian, 1959), p. 53.

6. *Ibid.*, p. 52.

7. *Ibid.*, p. 72.

8. Mircea Eliade, *Cosmos and History: The Myth of the Eternal Return*, pp. 104, 105.

9. *Ibid.*, pp. 111–12.

10. Auerbach, *op. cit.*, p. 72.

11. *Ibid.*

12. Eliade, *op. cit.*, p. 129.

13. *Ibid.*, pp. 129–30.

14. Martial Rose, ed., *The Wakefield Mystery Plays* (Garden City, N.Y.: Doubleday, 1963), p. 59.

15. Line numberings follow those of the Folger Library General Reader's Shakespeare, Louis B. Wright & Virginia A. LaMar, eds., *The Tragedy of King Lear* (New York: Washington Square Press, 1967).

16. *Agamemnon*, ll. 177–178.

17. *Ibid.*, ll. 47–49.

18. *Ibid.*, p. 23.

19. Quoted in *A New Variorum Edition of Shakespeare: King Lear*, ed. Horace Howard Furness (New York: Dover, 1963), p. 189.

20. Friedrich Nietzsche, *The Birth of Tragedy and the Genealogy of Morals*, p. 29.

21. *Ibid.*

22. Jan Kott, *Shakespeare Our Contemporary*, trans. Boleslaw Taborski (Garden City, N.Y.: Doubleday, 1964), p. 105.

23. *Ibid.*, p. 104.

24. *Ibid.*

25. Nietzsche, *op. cit.*, p. 51.

26. *The Collected Poems of W. B. Yeats* (New York: Macmillan, 1956), p. 293.

27. Nietzsche, *op. cit.*, p. 52.

28. See *A New Variorum Edition of Shakespeare: King Lear*, pp. 467–78.

29. *Ibid.*, p. 477.

30. *Ibid.*

31. Kitto, *op. cit.*, p. 335.

32. *The Confessions of St. Augustine*, trans. Rex Warner (New York: Mentor-Omega, 1963), pp. 150, 153.

33. See, for example, the drawing of the Valenciennes Passion Play of 1547 in Sheldon Cheney, *The Theatre: Three Thousand Years of Drama, Acting and Stagecraft* (New York: Longmans, 1952), p. 154.

34. See n. 12 above.

35. Quoted in William Barrett, *Irrational Man: A Study in Existential Philosophy* (Garden City, N.Y.: Doubleday, 1958), p. 26.

36. Eliade, *op. cit.*, p. 54.

37. Nietzsche, *op. cit.*, p. 38.

The Tragedy of Historical Man: From Hegel to Ibsen

1. Mircea Eliade, *Cosmos and History: The Myth of the Eternal Return*, pp. 145–46.

2. Carl L. Becker, *The Heavenly City of the Eighteenth-Century Philosophers* (New Haven: Yale Paperbound, 1965).

3. Toulmin and Goodfield (New York: Harper, 1965), pp. 233, 235.

4. Georg Wilhelm Friedrich Hegel, *The Philosophy of History*, trans. J. Sibree (New York: Dover, 1956), pp. 30–31.

5. Eric Bentley, *The Playwright as Thinker: A Study of Drama in Modern Times* (New York: Meridian, 1957), p. 28; Robert Brustein, *The Theatre of Revolt: An Approach to Modern Drama* (Boston: Little, 1965), p. 62.

6. Hegel, *The Philosophy of History*, pp. 9, 23.

7. *Ibid.*, pp. 16–18.

8. *Ibid.*, p. 17.

9. *Ibid.*, p. 39.

10. *Ibid.*, p. 29.

11. Nietzsche, *The Birth of Tragedy and the Genealogy of Morals*, pp. 78–79.

12. A. J. Ayer, selections in William Barrett & Henry D. Aiken, eds., *Philos-*

ophy in the Twentieth Century: An Anthology (New York: Random House, 1962), pp. 52–74, 87–101 passim.

13. E. R. Dodds, The Greeks and the Irrational, p. 183.

14. Nietzsche, op. cit., p. 92.

15. Ibid., p. 95.

16. George Steiner, The Death of Tragedy (New York: Hill & Wang, 1963), p. 84.

17. Stendhal, Racine and Shakespeare, trans. Guy Daniels (New York: Crowell-Collier, 1962); see, for example, Victor Hugo's "Preface to Cromwell," in Barrett H. Clark, ed., European Theories of the Drama (New York: Crown, 1947), pp. 368–81.

18. N. Joseph Calarco, "Tragedy as Demonstration," Educational Theatre Journal, XVIII, No. 3 (October, 1966), 271–74; Francis Fergusson, The Idea of a Theatre, A Study of Ten Plays: The Art of Drama in Changing Perspective (Garden City, N.Y.: Doubleday, 1954), p. 62.

19. Jean Racine, "Preface to Phèdre," in Clark, op. cit., p. 157.

20. Jean Racine, Phaedra, trans. Robert Henderson, in Paul Landis, ed., Six Plays by Corneille and Racine (New York: Modern Library, 1931), p. 251.

21. Aristotle, The Nichomachean Ethics, trans. W. D. Ross, in Richard McKeon, ed., The Basic Works of Aristotle (New York: Random House, 1941), 1109^b:1–5.

22. Phaedra, p. 252.

23. Hippolytus, ll. 191–92; Phaedra, p. 254.

24. Phaedra, p. 258.

25. Ibid., p. 260.

26. Ibid., pp. 271, 272, 274.

27. Becker, op. cit., pp. 102–3.

28. Phaedra, pp. 285, 278.

29. Hippolytus, ll. 1105–50.

30. Phaedra, p. 289.

31. Ibid., p. 300.

32. Ibid., pp. 303, 302.

33. Fergusson, op. cit., pp. 62–63.

34. Phyllis Hartnoll, ed., The Oxford Companion to the Theatre, 2nd ed. (London: Oxford University Press, 1957), pp. 360, 656.

35. Friedrich Hebbel, "Preface to Maria Magdalena," trans. Carl Richard Mueller, in Robert W. Corrigan, ed., The Modern Theatre (New York: Macmillan, 1964), p. 22.

36. Bentley, op. cit., pp. 23–25.

37. Hebbel, "Preface to Maria Magdalena," pp. 23, 24.

38. Ibid., pp. 21, 20.

39. T. M. Campbell, The Life and Works of Friedrich Hebbel (Boston: R. G. Badger, 1919), p. 110.

40. Hebbel, "Preface to Maria Magdalena," p. 20.

41. Hebbel, "A Word about the Drama," trans. Carl Richard Mueller, in Corrigan, op. cit., pp. 24–25.

42. Quoted in Bentley, op. cit., p. 30.

43. Hebbel, "A Word about the Drama," p. 24.

44. Hebbel, "Preface to Maria Magdalena," p. 21.

45. Hegel, The Philosophy of History, pp. 29–33.

46. Hebbel, Maria Magdalena, in Corrigan, op. cit., p. 37.

47. Ibid., pp. 39–40.

48. Ibid., p. 41.

49. Ibid., p. 47.

50. Ibid., pp. 32, 35, 38.

51. Ibid., p. 41.

52. Ibid., p. 48.

53. Ibid.

54. Etienne Gilson, The Unity of Philosophical Experience (New York: Scribners, 1937), p. 245.

55. See n. 15 above.

56. Hermann J. Weigand, The Modern Ibsen (New York: Dutton, 1960), pp. 276, 299.

57. Joseph T. Shipley, ed., Dictionary of World Literature, Criticism, Forms, Technique (Paterson, N.J.: Littlefield, 1964), p. 149.

58. Fergusson, op. cit., p. 170.

59. Henrik Ibsen, The Master Builder, in Six Plays, trans. Eva Le Gallienne (New York: Modern Library, 1957), p. 432.

60. Ibid., pp. 435–36.

61. Ibid., p. 444.

62. Ibid., p. 446.

63. Ibid., pp. 447–48.
64. Ibid., p. 449.
65. Ibid., p. 453.
66. Ibid., p. 455.
67. Ibid., p. 457.
68. Ibid., pp. 458, 459.
69. Ibid., p. 460.
70. Ibid., p. 473.
71. Ibid., pp. 474–76.
72. Ibid., p. 479.
73. Ibid., p. 480.
74. Ibid., pp. 480–81.
75. Ibid., p. 484.
76. Ibid., p. 492.
77. Ibid., p. 501.
78. Ibid., pp. 504–6.
79. Nietzsche, op. cit., pp. 51, 31.
80. The Master Builder, pp. 508–10.

Two Modern Playwrights; Conclusions

1. The epigraph for this chapter is from The Collected Poems of W. B. Yeats (New York: Macmillan, 1956), p. 236.
2. Emile Zola, "Preface to Thérèse Raquin," in Barrett H. Clark, ed., European Theories of the Drama, p. 400.
3. Martin Esslin, Brecht: The Man and His Work (Garden City, N.Y.: Doubleday, 1960), p. 232.
4. Bertolt Brecht, "On the Experimental Theatre," trans. Carl Richard Mueller, Tulane Drama Review, VI, No. 1 (September, 1961), 9.
5. Ibid., pp. 12–13.
6. Ibid., p. 14.
7. Mircea Eliade, Cosmos and History: The Myth of the Eternal Return, p. 149.
8. Bertolt Brecht, The Mother; with Notes by the Author, trans. Lee Baxandall (New York: Grove, 1965), pp. 114, 131.
9. Brecht on Theatre: The Development of an Aesthetic (New York: Hill & Wang, 1964), p. 220.
10. Ibid., p. 221.
11. Bertolt Brecht, Mother Courage, trans. Eric Bentley, in his The Modern Theatre, Vol. II (Garden City, N.Y.: Doubleday, 1955), pp. 301, 304.
12. Ibid., p. 243.
13. Ibid., p. 313.
14. Martin Esslin, The Theatre of the Absurd (Garden City, N.Y.: Doubleday, 1961).
15. Jean-Paul Sartre, Saint Genet: Actor and Martyr, trans. Bernard Frechtman (New York: Braziller, 1963), pp. 24, 26.
16. Jean Genet, The Screens, trans. Bernard Frechtman (New York: Grove, 1962), p. 13.
17. Ibid., p. 42; The Maids and Deathwatch, trans. Bernard Frechtman (New York: Grove, 1954), p. 61.
18. The Screens, p. 97.
19. Ibid., p. 81.
20. Ibid., p. 135.
21. Sartre, op. cit., p. 27.
22. The Screens, pp. 31, 188.
23. Ibid., pp. 189, 190.
24. Ibid., pp. 192–93, 197–99.
25. Ibid., p. 201.
26. Sartre, op. cit., p. 24.
27. Richard B. Sewall, "The Tragic Form," in Michel & Sewall, Tragedy: Modern Essays in Criticism, p. 120.
28. William Barrett, Irrational Man: A Study in Existential Philosophy, p. 83.
29. Federico García Lorca, Blood Wedding, in Three Tragedies, trans. James Graham-Luján & Richard L. O'Connell (New York: New Directions, 1955), p. 99.
30. Nietzsche, The Birth of Tragedy and the Genealogy of Morals, p. 139.
31. Hegel on Tragedy, ed. Anne & Henry Paolucci (Garden City, N.Y.: Doubleday, 1962), p. 71.
32. Emile Zola, "The Novel as Social Science," trans. Belle M. Sherman, in Richard Ellman & Charles Feidelson, Jr., eds., The Modern Tradition: Backgrounds of Modern Literature (New York: Oxford University Press, 1965), pp. 278, 277.
33. Etienne Gilson, The Unity of Philosophical Experience, p. 284.
34. Nietzsche, op. cit., p. 95.

·WORKS CITED IN THE TEXT·

Aristotle. *Aristotle's Theory of Poetry and Fine Art*, 4th ed., ed. & trans. S. H. Butcher. New York: Dover, 1951.

Aristotle. *The Basic Works of Aristotle*, ed. Richard McKeon. New York: Random House, 1941.

Arrowsmith, William. "The Criticism of Greek Tragedy," *Tulane Drama Review*, III, No. 3 (Spring, 1959), 31–57.

Arrowsmith, William. "A Greek Theatre of Ideas," *Arion*, II, No. 3 (Autumn, 1963), 32–56.

Auerbach, Erich. *Scenes from the Drama of European Literature: Six Essays*. New York: Meridian, 1959.

Augustine. *The Confessions of St. Augustine*, trans. Rex Warner. New York: New American Library (Mentor-Omega), 1963.

Barrett, William. *Irrational Man: A Study in Existential Philosophy*. Garden City, N.Y.: Doubleday, 1958; Doubleday Anchor, 1962.

Barrett, William, & Henry D. Aiken, eds. *Philosophy in the Twentieth Century: An Anthology*, text ed.; 2 Vols. New York: Random House, 1962.

Becker, Carl L. *The Heavenly City of the Eighteenth-Century Philosophers*. New Haven: Yale University Press, 1932; Yale Paperbound, 1965.

Bentley, Eric. *The Playwright as Thinker: A Study of Drama in Modern Times*. New York: Meridian, 1957.

Brecht, Bertolt. *Brecht on Theatre: The Development of an Aesthetic*, ed. & trans. John Willet. New York: Hill & Wang, 1964.

Brecht, Bertolt. *The Mother; with Notes by the Author*, trans. Lee Baxandall. New York: Grove, 1965.

Brecht, Bertolt. *Mother Courage*, trans. Eric Bentley, in Eric Bentley, ed., *The Modern Theatre: II*. Garden City, N.Y.: Doubleday Anchor, 1955.

Brecht, Bertolt. "On the Experimental Theatre," trans. Carl Richard Mueller, *Tulane Drama Review*, VI, No. 1 (September, 1961), 3–17.

Brustein, Robert. *The Theatre of Revolt: An Approach to the Modern Drama*. Boston: Little, 1965.

Bury, J. B. *A History of Greece to the Death of Alexander the Great*. London: Macmillan, 1913; New York: Random House (Modern Library), 1937.

Calarco, N. Joseph. "Tragedy as Demonstration," *Educational Theatre Journal*, XVIII, No. 3 (October, 1966), 271–274.

Campbell, T. M. *The Life and Works of Friedrich Hebbel*. Boston: R. G. Badger, 1919.

Cheney, Sheldon. *The Theatre: Three Thousand Years of Drama, Acting and Stagecraft*. New York: Longmans, 1952.

Clark, Barrett H., ed. *European Theories of the Drama*. New York: Crown, 1947.

Corrigan, Robert W., ed. *The Modern Theatre*. New York: Macmillan, 1964.

DeWitt, Norman J. "The Ars Poetica of Horace," *Drama Survey*, I, No. 2 (Fall, 1961), 149–64.

Dodds, E. R. *The Greeks and the Irrational*. Boston: Beacon Press, 1951; Berkeley: University of California Press, 1956.

Eliade, Mircea. *Cosmos and History: The Myth of the Eternal Return*, trans. Willard R. Trask. New York: Pantheon Books, 1954; Harper Torchbooks, 1959.

Ellman, Richard, & Charles Feidelson, Jr., eds. *The Modern Tradition: Backgrounds of Modern Literature*. New York: Oxford University Press, 1965.

Esslin, Martin. *Brecht: The Man and his Work*. London: 1959; Garden City, N.Y.: Doubleday, 1960.

Esslin, Martin. *The Theatre of the Absurd*. Garden City, N.Y.: Doubleday Anchor, 1961.

Fergusson, Francis. *The Idea of a Theatre, A Study of Ten Plays: The Art of Drama in Changing Perspective*. Princeton, N.J.: Princeton University Press, 1949; New York: Doubleday Anchor, 1954.

Genet, Jean. *The Maids* and *Deathwatch*, trans. Bernard Frechtman. New York: Grove, 1954.

Genet, Jean. *The Screens*, trans. Bernard Frechtman. New York: Grove, 1962.

Gilson, Etienne. *The Unity of Philosophical Experience*. New York: Scribners, 1937.

Grene, David, & Richmond Lattimore, eds. *The Complete Greek Tragedies*, Vols. I–VII. New York: Modern Library, n.d.; *Greek Tragedies*, Vols. I–III. Chicago: University of Chicago Press (Phoenix), 1960.

Hartnoll, Phyllis, ed. *The Oxford Companion to the Theatre*, 2nd ed. London: Oxford University Press, 1957.

Hegel, Georg Wilhelm Friedrich. *Hegel on Tragedy*, ed. Anne & Henry Paolucci. Garden City, N.Y.: Doubleday Anchor, 1962.

Hegel, Georg Wilhelm Friedrich. *The Philosophy of History*, trans. J. Sibree. New York: Wiley, 1944; Dover, 1956.

The Holy Bible, King James Version.

Hurrell, John Dennis. "The Figural Approach to Medieval Drama," *College English*, XXVI, No. 8 (May, 1965), 598–604.

Ibsen, Henrik. *Six Plays*, trans. Eva Le Gallienne. New York: Random House (Modern Library), 1951, 1957.

Jaeger, Werner. *Paideia: The Ideals of Greek Culture*, 3 vols., trans. Gilbert Highet. Oxford: Blackwell, 1939; New York: Oxford University Press, 1962.

Jones, Ernest. *Hamlet and Oedipus*. New York: Norton, 1949; Garden City, N.Y.: Doubleday Anchor, 1954. Revision of "The Oedipus-Complex as an Explanation of Hamlet's Mystery: A Study in Motive," *American Journal of Psychology*, XXI (1910), 72–113.

Kitto, H. D. F. *Form and Meaning in Drama: A Study of Six Greek Plays and of Hamlet*. London: Methuen, 1956; New York: Barnes & Noble, 1957; University Paperbacks, 1960.

Knight, G. Wilson. *The Wheel of Fire: Essays in Interpretation of Shakespeare's Sombre Tragedies*. London: Oxford University Press, 1930; 5th rev. ed., New York: Meridian, 1957.

Kott, Jan. *Shakespeare Our Contemporary*, trans. Boleslaw Taborski. Garden City, N.Y.: Doubleday, 1964.

Lorca, Federico García. *Three Tragedies: Blood Wedding, Yerma, Bernarda Alba*, trans. James Graham-Luján & Richard L. O'Connell. New York: New Directions, 1955.

Michel, Laurence, & Richard B. Sewall, eds. *Tragedy: Modern Essays in Criticism*. Englewood Cliffs, N.J.: Prentice-Hall, 1963.

Nietzsche, Friedrich. *The Birth of Tragedy and the Genealogy of Morals*, trans. Francis Golffing. Garden City, N.Y.: Doubleday Anchor, 1956.

Plato. *The Collected Dialogues of Plato, Including the Letters*, ed. Edith Hamilton & Huntington Cairns. New York: Pantheon, 1963.

Racine, Jean, & Pierre Corneille. *Six Plays by Corneille and Racine*, ed. Paul Landis. New York: Modern Library, 1931, 1959.

Rose, Martial, ed. *The Wakefield Mystery Plays*. London: Evans Brothers, 1961; Garden City, N.Y.: Doubleday Anchor, 1963.

Runes, Dagobert D., ed. *Dictionary of Philosophy*. Ames, Ia., Paterson, N.J.: Littlefield, 1955, 1964.

Sartre, Jean-Paul. *Saint Genet: Actor and Martyr*, trans. Bernard Frechtman. New York: Braziller, 1963.

Schechner, Richard. "Approaches to Theory/Criticism," *Tulane Drama Review*, X, No. 4 (Summer, 1966), 20–53.

Shakespeare, William. *A New Variorum Edition of Shakespeare: King Lear*, ed. Horace Howard Furness. New York: Dover, 1963.

Shakespeare, William. *The Tragedy of King Lear*, in Louis B. Wright & Virginia A. LaMar, eds., *The Folger Library General Reader's Shakespeare*. New York: Washington Square Press, 1957, 1967.

Shipley, Joseph T., ed. *Dictionary of World Literature, Criticism, Forms, Technique*. New York: Philosophical Library, 1953; Paterson, N.J.: Littlefield, 1964.

Steiner, George. *The Death of Tragedy*. New York: Knopf, 1961; Hill & Wang Dramabook, 1963.

Stendhal. *Racine and Shakespeare*, trans. Guy Daniels. New York: Crowell-Collier, 1962.

Thucydides. *The Peloponnesian War*, trans. Rex Warner. Baltimore: Penguin Books, 1954.

Toulmin, Stephen, & June Goodfield. *The Discovery of Time*. New York: Harper, 1965.

Weigand, Hermann J. *The Modern Ibsen: A Reconsideration*. New York: Holt, 1925; Dutton Paperback, 1960.

Yeats, William Butler. *The Collected Poems of W. B. Yeats*. New York: Macmillan, 1956.

· INDEX ·

TRAGIC BEING

Apollo and Dionysus in Western Drama

BY N. JOSEPH CALARCO

Focused on a dozen plays by nine play-wrights, this is a study of tragedy in Western drama from classic to modern times. The author explores the hidden order beyond tragedy's visible circle of action and suffering, and the value which that order assigns to human existence.

The plays examined are Aeschylus' trilogy the *Oresteia*, Sophocles' *Oedipus at Colonus*, Euripides' *Hippolytus* and *Bacchae*, Shakespeare's *King Lear*, Racine's *Phèdre*, Hebbel's *Maria Magdalena*, Ibsen's *The Master Builder*, Brecht's *Mother Courage*, and Genet's *The Screens*. These plays, as the author shows, pose the tragic dilemma in particularly vivid and forceful terms.

In his introduction Professor Calarco defines two related concepts on which